THE MAGIC OF SELF-CONFIDENCE

by Daniel Meacham

Produced by The Miller Press, Inc.

A FIRESIDE BOOK
Published by Simon & Schuster, Inc.
NEW YORK

Copyright © 1984 by The Miller Press, Inc.
All rights reserved
including the right of reproduction
in whole or in part in any form
A Fireside Book
Published by Simon & Schuster, Inc.
Simon & Schuster Building
Rockefeller Center
1230 Avenue of the Americas
New York, New York 10020
FIRESIDE and colophon are registered trademarks of Simon & Schuster, Inc.
Designed by Stanley S. Drate/Folio Graphics Co. Inc.
Manufactured in the United States of America
Printed and bound by Fairfield Graphics
10 9 8 7 6 5 4 3 2 1

Library of Congress Cataloging in Publication Data
Meacham, Daniel.
  The magic of self-confidence.
  "A Fireside book."
  1. Self-confidence. I. Title.
BF575.S39M43   1984   158'.1   84-13983
ISBN 0-671-54193-5

*To Susan and Jacob
and all the kids
with confidence and love*

CONTENTS

1
The Little Engine That Could　　11

2
The Circle of Self-Confidence　　21

3
The Self-Confidence Test　　31

4
Going the Distance　　59

5
The Art of Self-Confidence, the Business of Success   69

6
For Women Only. Mouseburger and Miss America: Models of Self-Confidence   79

7
Life's Scenarios   91

8
What Other Authors Have Written That Can Help You   113

9
Coming to Terms   121

THE MAGIC OF SELF-CONFIDENCE

1
The Little Engine That Could

*T*here's one in every crowd. The man wh[o]
the life of every party. The woman who's the first to [get]
the job she wants, first to get a raise, first to get [a]
promotion, and off to a running start in her career. T[he]
guy who has no more athletic ability than you, but bea[ts]
you nine out of ten times on the tennis court. The g[irl]
who has more dates, more boyfriends than she know[s]
what to do with. The people with the powerful personal[i]ties and winning attitudes.

Who are these people, anyway? You've seen them, yo[u]
can't help watching them and remembering who the[y]
are. They stand out in a crowd. They seem charmed[,]
blessed with something special. They are perfectly re[-]

The Magic of Self-Confidence

laxed, possess a certain ease and charisma, and are secure in who they are and what they want. You see them and the first thing you say to yourself is, "There goes someone who has the world on a string, a person who's bound for success." Then, if you're a normal, healthy, achievement-oriented individual, the next thing you say to yourself is, "What do they have that I don't?"

The answer is simple: They have self-confidence. What's startling is this: The reason they are special, the reason they are winners, is that they made a conscious decision to be so. They made a promise to themselves and kept it. It's one of the easiest promises to make, and without some support (the kind I'm going to give you) one of the hardest to keep.

The fact is, *you* can have self-confidence for the asking. With a little work, a little practice, and a whole lot of determination, you can earn that mark of distinction—you can develop the confidence you need to achieve excellence. *But you have to want it to get it!*

Charm. Charisma. Self-confidence. The very words have a magical quality about them, a mystique of prestige and power. They are the words we use to describe the men and women we most admire. They bespeak accomplishment, savvy, and skill. But as magical as self-confidence is, you *don't* have to work magic to attain it. The key is a deep and driving desire to reap its benefits. You have to formulate a plan of action and stick to it, organize your life in such a way that a sense of confidence will come naturally. The key is determination.

Look at it this way: Everyone has muscles and everyone uses them. Otherwise, we'd never get anywhere. Some people, however, use their muscles better than others. If you are willing to work them, to exercise regularly and follow a sensible, ongoing program of mus-

The Little Engine That Could

cle development, you naturally become healthier and much more attuned to your body. If not, your muscles atrophy and lose their shape and vitality. The same is true of self-confidence. If you are willing to go all the way, to make a commitment and put your heart into it, then and only then can you shed the fat of self-doubt and realize a more assured, more secure, more confident you. The more you harness your innate strengths and abilities, the stronger you become mentally and emotionally. Suddenly, you are the one who stands out in a crowd, the one who walks with that aura of prestige and that quiet, wonderful feeling of purpose and power. You are the image of a winner!

That's what this book is all about: how to tone and how to flex the muscles of your self-confidence.

As you read this book, the most important thing to remember (it's a very easy thing to forget) is this: Self-confidence is not something someone gives you. It is something inside you, something waiting to be discovered and cultivated and fortified. You already have the seeds of self-confidence; this book will help you make them grow.

What you have to do, what I will help you do—with confidence-building exercises, tips to guide you through specific situations, and some real-life models and examples—is reach down inside yourself and bring that inner core of strength to the surface. It's the act that runners call "digging down." Of course it will take time and energy—everything worth having does—but there's no doubt that once you *decide* to do it, you *can* do it. And once you've grabbed hold, once you have tapped that inner reserve and feel that magical quality turning your life around, you'll never regret the work you put into finding your emotional muscle. Your investment will

The Magic of Self-Confidence

pay a lifetime of rich and dynamic dividends in both your personal life and your career.

Nothing in the world succeeds like self-confidence. And there's no limit to what it can do for you and help you do for yourself. You are in total command of the forces that shape your life and your future. Wherever you go, whatever you do, whatever you want to accomplish, if you have confidence in yourself, you're sure to be a winner.

From raising a family to raising your golf score, from enlivening your love life to lighting a fire under your career, having self-confidence in your corner is like making a friend and ally out of Lady Fortune. But what we commonly call chance or the luck of the draw is, more often than not, having the composure and the discipline to make the right moves at the right times. In other words, you have to learn *how* to be lucky, learn how to control your destiny. You'll be amazed as you begin to put into practice what you read in this book how things begin to happen the way you want them to, how things seem suddenly to fall into place. Your ideas gain new respect and more of your plans are realized.

It's like stacking the deck in your favor—and in the game of life, self-confidence is a royal flush. Nothing beats it and no one can take it away. Once you've got it in your hand, there's no other feeling quite like it: knowing you're a winner, knowing you've beaten the odds.

Which is not to say you're going to win the pot of gold every time out—no one can. Not only is it impossible, but it would be boring. It's the *feeling* of confidence that counts. Consider someone like baseball slugger Reggie Jackson, a man whose middle name is confidence. When he goes up to bat, he's not thinking "three swings and I'm

The Little Engine That Could

out," he's thinking one swing is all it takes to win a game. Of course he's not going to win a game with every swing of the bat—the game would be pointless if he did—but he's going to win a lot more games than the guy who's afraid to even swing for fear of striking out.

Winners are people who know how to lose, who can lose knowing that eventually they'll win. They are people who, no matter how many times they strike out, know that as sure as day follows night, it's only a matter of time before they blast that game-winning home run. (Reggie Jackson, by the way, has struck out more times than any other player in the history of Major League baseball; he is also known as Mr. October, because of his talent for playing under pressure and leading so many of his teams into the World Series.) Belief in your own abilities—even after striking out—is the force behind self-confidence.

Contrary to what you might believe (and contrary to what some people would like you to believe), you don't have to become a Zen master, learn self-hypnosis, or pay $50 an hour to some "professional" self-confidence builder. *You* can make the decisions, and *you* can take the initiative. It's that simple! If you feel that Zen or something similar will help relax or fulfill you, take advantage of it. But first you must have a clear idea of what you're doing and why you're doing it. The sensible, straightforward guidelines in this book are designed to give you a foundation upon which to build. But there's no magic formula here; the magic is in *you*.

A couple of things to keep in mind before we get started:

First: Never give up. Once you have set your sights on this or any goal, don't be discouraged by setbacks. It's what I call the *little-engine-that-could principle*—if you

The Magic of Self-Confidence

think you can, you can. Everyone experiences setbacks, but those who work through and get over them reach the top of the mountain. What stands between mediocrity and excellence, between just getting by and attaining fulfillment, between failure and success is the small but powerful voice within you that won't say, "I can't do it." You can do it, and you will do it!

Second: Never second-guess yourself. Never get caught in the mind-boggling but tempting labyrinth of the three Rs: reassessment . . . repetition . . . and regret. It's much easier to get into the maze than to get out, and all you'll ever find within is paralysis. Don't let what happened yesterday inhibit what *is* happening today or *will* happen tomorrow. It's ancient history, and nothing you can do will change it. Stick to the present and the future; look to the past only when you can do it rationally and objectively as a way to improve on the other two. Don't say, "I wish I had done it differently"; say, "Next time I *will* do it differently!"

Now, there is a school of thought that says, if you dwell on your past it will make your future easier. I don't buy that. It's like driving from New York to California with your car set in reverse. Sure, you might get there, but there are easier ways to do it. The bottom line: Keep your eye on the road, and use your rearview mirror only to avoid trouble.

So let's rev up the little engine that could and get started!

In the next chapters, I'm going to show you how to overcome your doubts; how to find the power to take charge and win in your career, in athletic competition, and in your personal life; how to organize yourself, order your priorities, and get done the things you've always

The Little Engine That Could

wanted to get done; how to impress and influence people and enhance your prestige. In a word, how to command respect.

We're headed down the road to self-confidence—a road that leads straight to success. Before you know it, you and the people around you will feel the beautiful magic and the mystery of *your* self-confidence.

2
The Circle of Self-Confidence

"We do not run away because we are afraid
but are afraid because we run away."
—B. F. SKINNER

*B*efore we go any further I want to give you a basic framework from which to build—a conceptual model to help you understand and visualize the psychology of self-confidence. Once you have an idea of the mechanisms of everyday life that raise and lower your self-confidence level, you will be in a position to manipulate those mechanisms, to improve your self-awareness and fortify your self-esteem. The model is called the "Circle of Self-Confidence." Through its simple graphic design you will see how to develop, nurture, and sustain an enduring sense of personal well-being and poise. In this chapter you will learn the fundamentals of the

The Magic of Self-Confidence

Circle: what defines it and how it works. In subsequent chapters I will demonstrate how to get *into* the Circle—how to get on and stay on its track. I will show you how to take advantage of it in specific situations and to incorporate it into the engine that drives you to success.

First, let's take a look at a common misconception that could discourage you from proceeding. It's the belief that self-confidence is not something one acquires but something one is blessed with; that, like blond hair, blue eyes, or a family estate, you're either born with it or you're not. Many of us have the tendency to take the easy out here. We tell ourselves that self-confidence is a force beyond our control, and that its advantages are endowed, as if by lottery, on a chosen few. In this regard confidence is like money: If you know how the marketplace works, if you know what investments to make, if you know what to do and when to do it, you don't need a rich uncle to make your fortune.

A very successful buyer of European fashions for one of Fifth Avenue's posh department stores told me: "I was a quiet, shy little girl. I stayed pretty much to myself. If you had known me you would have said I was one of the most unassuming and unambitious kids you'd ever met. My parents used to worry about me, even though they tried not to show it. As I got older they would invite boys from the neighborhood over to our house—I'm sure they felt they'd better marry me off quick, because *someone* would have to take care of me! But I had a secret, something that kept me going. I loved to pore over my mother's magazines, and then sit at the sewing machine and try to copy the clothes in the ads. I wasn't too successful at the time, but I knew somewhere deep down inside that as long as I could play 'dress-up' in my life, I would be happy. As I look back on it I realize that even then my vocation was growing, by fits and starts, within

The Circle of Self-Confidence

me. Eventually, every decision I made was directed toward getting to where you see me now.

"Not to say it was a piece of cake—it wasn't! When, after finishing school, I finally threw caution to the wind and headed for New York, I was still just a frightened little girl. But the important thing is that once I made my decision to work toward this goal, I gave myself every opportunity to achieve it. When I recall my past insecurities I think of that old question about the glass of water: Is it half-empty or half-full? In my case it was half-full, and now *I'm* the woman responsible for the clothes in the magazine that other little girls dream about."

You do not acquire self-confidence overnight, you develop it with a systematic and ongoing process. This process is based on the snowball effect. A single act of confidence breeds a feeling of confidence in yourself that, in turn, breeds further and more ambitious acts of confidence. The process is like learning a language. At first you feel awkward and uncomfortable, and the words don't seem to fit in your mouth. You make silly mistakes, and even when you pronounce the words correctly you feel as if someone else is speaking them. But the more you practice, the easier it becomes and the more natural you feel. Before long you find that not only are you speaking in a new language, you are thinking in one as well. By *acting* self-confident you *become* self-confident—fluent in the language of success.

As with any language, the first thing to learn is the vocabulary—an elegant, concise, simple lexicon of just four words and phrases:

Stimulus . . . which is the specific action you take.
Response . . . which is the specific *re*action others have to you.

The Magic of Self-Confidence

Positive reinforcement and *negative reinforcement* . . . which are the two possible results of the stimulus/response equation.

In order to grasp the meaning of these words, let's examine the basic structure—the grammar—of our new language:

Imagine for a moment the world divided into two distinct zones. You occupy the first zone; and your environment, consisting of your friends, your family, your lover, your teachers, your boss, your competitors—in short, all the people in your life—occupies the second. Where these two zones meet, in the critical interaction between them, self-confidence either comes into being or goes out the window. The reason is that the level of your self-confidence naturally corresponds to how others perceive and deal with you. We all look to our surroundings for support and fulfillment.

Although both zones—you and your environment—play important roles in this arrangement, your role is the primary one. You are the leading player from whom all the other players take their cue. You *act*, your environment *reacts*; you provide the *stimulus*, your environment the *response*. You are the controlling agent, you are active—and unless you stimulate it, your environment remains passive and unresponsive. Your self-confident *act* elicits a *response* of respect from your environment. This respect is your *positive reinforcement*, which results in future, more pronounced acts of self-confidence. Likewise, an *un*self-confident act elicits an unfavorable response or none at all, which, as *negative reinforcement*, can discourage you and reduce your self-confidence level.

Clearly, the way we behave is often determined by the

The Circle of Self-Confidence

consequences of our past behavior. At times, however, you have to struggle against the tendency to let your past overwhelm your future. No matter how self-confident you are—and especially when you are in the process of *building* your self-confidence—you will experience setbacks. You may even fall flat on your face. You can't let it deter your forward momentum, you must forge ahead. The danger here is that if you act either unself-confidently *or* self-confidently and get negative results, your momentum may be broken. The fear is that once you're side-tracked from the Circle, you will not be able to get back on. Like a child learning how to walk, you have to learn how to fall down and get back up again.

A friend of mine recently decided to join a dance class—not to become a professional dancer, but to learn to unwind, work up a sweat, feel good about herself physically and emotionally. She wanted to move with confidence. For the first few weeks the class had just the opposite effect. She felt she couldn't keep up with the rest of the class, she felt awkward, clumsy, embarrassed, and came away from each hour-long session unhappy and dreading the next one. She could easily have quit on the spot—it certainly was the most appealing option at the moment. But she knew if she did, she would soon feel even worse. She would come down on herself with the words "Here's one more thing I can't do, one more example of my inadequacy." Instead, she picked herself up off the floor and determined not to surrender to her fears. By continuing to make the effort, by pushing herself beyond self-doubt, her body—and her mind—slowly started to come around. "It's funny," she said, "it came gradually, but it still had a tremendous impact on me. One week I felt clumsy and out of place, the next, I began to feel my body responding. There's only one word to describe the feeling: ecstasy . . . not only because I was making the moves, but because I had come face to face with my self-doubt and had overcome it. The whole experience thrilled me and continues to as I begin to master each new step. I feel powerful, I feel myself taking control. It's still hard, and sometimes I still have setbacks, but then at other times I feel like I'm on top of the world."

Someone else I know works in the public relations department of a large publishing house in midtown Manhattan. He freely admits that when he was promoted from administrative assistant to publicist, he was less than enthusiastic—he didn't feel he fit the role of public spokesperson. He found meeting with the press particularly uncomfortable. "I felt," he says, "that, like me, they were there only because it was part of their job. They asked questions, I answered them, and that was that. They went away bored and shrugging their shoulders—and I simply endured these meetings. I felt it was a punishment I had to withstand in order to collect my paycheck." But then, he says, by chance an issue arose—the publication by his company of a provocative book by a controversial author, about which he felt strongly. The meetings with the press on this front were considerably more lively and combative, and for the first time he was excited by the whole process. He was enjoying himself. "I got some great write-ups in the papers, the president of the company called me up to his office to congratulate me, and since then my relationship with the press has improved 100 percent." He discovered that his attitude toward his environment determined not only how it responded to him, but also how *he* would act toward *it* in the future.

The key is knowing how to condition your environ-

THE CIRCLE OF SELF-CONFIDENCE

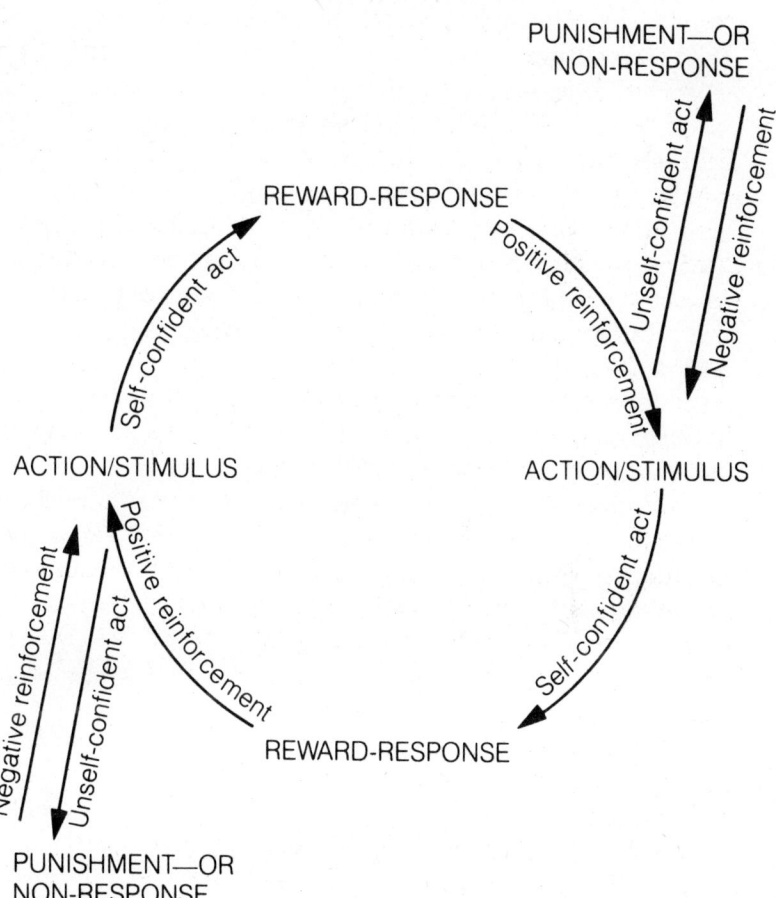

ment to respond favorably toward you (rather than learning by trial and error like our friend in public relations). If you *act* self-confidently, your environment, by perceiving you as such, rewards you for your trouble; that reward is the *positive reinforcement* of your behavior that you seek, and it increases the likelihood that you will act similarly in the future. In other words, first comes the act of self-confidence, *then* the feeling . . . It becomes a natural, flowing ongoing process.

Thus, the Circle of Self-Confidence.

The beauty of the Circle of Self-Confidence is that it is self-nourishing and builds its own momentum. A student, for example, who studies hard and does well on an exam feels the pleasure of his accomplishment, and will seek by continuing to study to recapture that pleasure. His high grades lead to greater opportunities in his career, and so on. Your single act of self-confidence—your determination to study harder, your decision to walk into your boss's office and ask for a raise, your insistence that your rights be recognized—starts that engine that propels you to success. The Circle of Self-Confidence, once set in motion, becomes an upward spiral of achievement.

3
The Self-Confidence Test

*I*n this chapter you have the opportunity to apply the theory of self-confidence from the previous chapter to real-life situations. There are sixteen questions, each representing a set of environmental conditions that might confront you in your career, your personal life, or your social life. You must decide how you would act in the particular situation, and choose from the three or four options offered.

The principle to keep in mind is this: How will the action you take reflect back on you? Remember, the point is to project yourself upon the environment so as to elicit a response that enhances your self-esteem. Also, take the long view: The action that seems easiest and most appropriate today may not be the one that pays dividends tomorrow.

The Magic of Self-Confidence

The test is designed to be difficult and to take into account the complexities and subtleties of real life. Furthermore, I don't pretend to have all the answers or to have covered all the bases; self-confidence is not something you can measure on a scale or hold in your hand—everyone has a different way of expressing it. If you disagree with me on one of the questions, and can justify the action you would take to your own satisfaction, then that's a point in your favor. The test is meant to give you a general idea of your current level of self-confidence. If you get just one, two or three questions right, then you are ready to set the Circle in motion.

The answers are at the end of the test, along with several paragraphs of text that explain why one option is preferred over the others. These notes are the real purpose of the quiz; they are designed so you can refer back to them in the future and apply them to your own life. Specific tips and suggestions are highlighted in bold type.

So, have fun with the test, and learn from it as well!

Questions

1. You are in an argument, and you know without a doubt that you are in the right. Your opponent refuses to concede the point. How do you respond?
   a) turn around and walk away; accept that there's nothing to be gained by going on
   b) stick to your guns; hold up your end until you get satisfaction
   c) admit the possibility that you are wrong

   YOUR ANSWER _____

The Self-Confidence Test

2. You are at a party and you see someone across the room you would like to get to know—maybe ask out for a date. But he or she seems deeply involved in conversation with others. What do you do?
   a) wait for the conversation to end, then introduce yourself
   b) find a mutual acquaintance to introduce you
   c) step right in and introduce yourself
   d) check out the conversation and, if appropriate, join in

   YOUR ANSWER _____

3. In a restaurant, you order a steak medium rare. It arrives at your table well done. To add insult to injury, your waiter claims that it's your fault. He says you ordered it well done, and shows you the order to prove it. He refuses to replace your steak. How do you deal with him?
   a) ask your fellow diners to confirm that you ordered it medium rare
   b) leave in protest, refusing to pay your bill
   c) chalk it up to experience, eat your steak, and resolve never to come to this place again
   d) ask to see the manager or maître d'

   YOUR ANSWER _____

The Magic of Self-Confidence

4. You are meeting someone for dinner at eight. This person is habitually late, and although you've made it clear before how much you despise waiting, it's past eight-thirty and there's still no sign of your date. What's the best course of action?
   a) let it go; accept the fact that your friend won't change
   b) get up and leave
   c) when your date arrives, forcefully restate your feelings and say this is the last time you'll wait
   d) wait to hear your date's excuse; then, if you don't buy it, leave

   YOUR ANSWER _____

5. You are in a movie theatre and the people behind you are talking. How do you deal with it?
   a) turn around and glare at them
   b) turn around and shush them, or ask them to stop
   c) get the usher
   d) leave, and get your money back on the way out

   YOUR ANSWER _____

The Self-Confidence Test

6. You're just starting a new job and your boss invites you to a company party after work. But you're not feeling well, you might be coming down with something. What do you do?
   a) offer apologies and go straight home
   b) ask him how important it is that you go to the party
   c) make an appearance and leave when you feel it's appropriate
   d) take some aspirin and show the boss what you're made of; stay at the party until the end

   YOUR ANSWER _____

7. You're out on a date with someone who's coming on much too strong. But it's someone you're very interested in, someone you don't want to turn off. How do you respond?
   a) tell your date you have to get up early and it's time you went home
   b) explain how you feel
   c) compromise, experiment; see what you feel comfortable with
   d) give in for the sake of the relationship

   YOUR ANSWER _____

The Magic of Self-Confidence

8. The other side of the coin: You are seeing someone for whom you feel a strong attraction; you are ready to take the relationship one more step, to realize a greater intimacy. How do you find out if your partner feels the same way?
   a) bring up the subject of intimacy in a general way and see what the person has to say
   b) explain how you feel
   c) try it: touch your partner affectionately and see what the response is

   YOUR ANSWER _____

9. You're in the market for a new set of speakers for your stereo, but you don't know much about the alternatives. In the showroom, you listen to two different speaker systems and the sound quality seems comparable; however, one set is priced $100 cheaper than the other. And as for the salesman, he might as well be speaking Greek. What do you decide to do?
   a) trust your instincts and buy the less expensive speakers
   b) find someone else in the store to help you
   c) forget this store and go somewhere else

   YOUR ANSWER _____

The Self-Confidence Test

10. You are faced with a situation (at a bank, a new job, or in school) during which you will be using a computer terminal. Although you've been told how to use it, you find working the machine confusing and uncomfortable. What's the best way to deal with it?
    a) request help
    b) keep trying, figuring that eventually it will get easier
    c) take a break and come back to it later
    d) curse the computer age

    YOUR ANSWER _____

11. You're in a business meeting and you introduce a proposal on which you have worked hard, and which you also believe will benefit your company. It is roundly criticized and finally rejected. What's your best course of action?
    a) analyze the criticism and try to find out why your proposal was rejected
    b) divide and conquer; seek out individuals from the meeting and try to change their minds
    c) go on to your next project

    YOUR ANSWER _____

The Magic of Self-Confidence

12. After buying some groceries, you stuff the change into your pocket and walk out of the store. Ten minutes later you pull the money out and find you've been shortchanged—enough to make you angry. What do you do?
    a) forget it; you have no way to prove it and chances are you won't get your money back
    b) go back, and, if necessary, make a stink about it
    c) write a letter of complaint to the store manager

    YOUR ANSWER _____

13. Tomorrow's a big day: You're going on a job interview, you're taking an important test, you're making an oral presentation. Although you know your stuff, you don't quite feel at ease. What should you do?
    a) get to bed early so you'll feel rested and ready
    b) see a movie, read a trashy novel, or meet some friends for dinner
    c) go over your material until you feel perfectly at ease

    YOUR ANSWER _____

The Self-Confidence Test

14. There's someone with whom you're very interested in going out. But each of the three or four times you've suggested meeting for drinks or dinner, all you've gotten for your trouble are excuses and apologies. What's your next move?
   a) give it up, you're wasting your energy
   b) ask straight out: "Are you interested in getting together or not?"
   c) ask the person to have lunch or brunch or a quick cup of coffee with you

   YOUR ANSWER _____

15. You've gone out with someone a couple of times and the relationship has developed quickly: You feel good about it, it feels right. But all of a sudden, overnight, the other person's attitude seems to have changed—maybe the phone calls have stopped, or you're getting together less frequently. What do you do?
   a) try to figure out what you did wrong
   b) ask straight out: "What's wrong, what's changed?"
   c) go with the flow, wait for the person to come around
   d) write if off, you can live without the aggravation

   YOUR ANSWER _____

The Magic of Self-Confidence

And now, the Ten-Point Bonus Question:

16. Finally, a general question: You've made an error in judgment (everyone does at one point or another)—you said something you wish you hadn't, you missed an appointment, you screwed up at work or at school. How do you respond?
    a) explain to those involved why it happened
    b) as soon as you realize your mistake, own up, take the blame
    c) let it pass, it happens to everyone

    YOUR ANSWER _____

The Self-Confidence Test

Answers

QUESTION **1: The Argument.**
Correct answer C

Walking away from an unsettled argument is rarely the way to go; it's a desperation measure, a last resort. If you felt strongly enough to argue in the first place, then throwing up your hands and shaking your head won't do any good. It's too much like surrender. Chances are, if you're walking away from an argument, you're walking away angry, frustrated, or bitter. Getting into an argument means you've already made an emotional investment—don't write off your investment so easily. If you're in for a penny, you're in for a pound.

And talk about frustration: Sticking to your guns until the bitter end is bad news! You could end up arguing until the polar icecaps melt and *still* not get any satisfaction. You might as well beat your head against the wall. You're wasting your breath, and more than likely, stiffening your opponent's obstinacy.

Now, for the perfect solution: Concede! Concede not that you're wrong, but the *possibility* that you might be wrong. It's a strategy guaranteed to disarm your opponent. It's like hitting a perfect tennis lob over his head, forcing him to retreat and reassess his position. It's also a way of setting the Circle of Self-Confidence in motion for better results in your *next* argument. Instead of pressing your position, you compel your opponent to defend *his* position. All you have to do is ask questions: He will see the argument in a new light, a light favorable to you (it's a device perfected by Socrates, a not-too-shabby debater himself). The point is this: If you have confidence in yourself, you won't feel the need to show your opponent

The Magic of Self-Confidence

up, to show that *you're* right and *he's* wrong. The almost certain result of your open-minded attitude is that your opponent bends, perhaps even concedes—and you win the point!

QUESTION 2: **Getting to Know You.**
Correct answer <u>D</u>

Waiting for a situation to develop in your favor is out of the question. It's nice when things fall in your lap, but never depend upon it. **You have to create your own opportunities.** You provide the stimulus that elicits a rewarding response. Asking someone else to make the introduction for you is also ill advised. Why get a third party involved? It only makes getting to know someone more complicated. You can't be sure, for instance, that you'll be introduced the way you want to be. (Of course there are exceptions to every rule: There are times when the only way to meet someone is through another person. But, again, it's a last resort.) **Never let someone else do what you can do better.**

So, introduce yourself. But never, under any circumstances, barge in and interrupt a conversation to do so. There's a big difference between being assertive and being aggressive. Pushy, aggressive people are far less sure of themselves than they appear—they try much too hard. Participating in the conversation, joining in, is an entirely different story. Expressing an interest in what other people have to say bespeaks self-confidence; you don't feel the need to be the center of attention, you don't require constant reassurance. And if you want to get to know someone, there's no better way to get that person interested in you than to show an interest in him or her.

The Self-Confidence Test

QUESTION 3: The Case of the Overcooked Steak.
Correct answer <u>D</u>

First of all, *never* shrug off something like this, consoling yourself by saying you won't frequent the place in the future. Whenever you pay your hard-earned money and expect that a service be performed in return, you have every right in the world to have that service done to your satisfaction. Furthermore, once you start telling yourself you won't frequent a place that doesn't live up to your expectations, it won't be long before you have no place left to go. **You have to watch out for your own interests**—because if you don't, no one else will.

Leaving in protest and refusing to pay your bill has a certain gut appeal, but it's a quick-lived pleasure. It will get you nowhere but aggravated, hungry, and out on the street looking for another place to eat. Leaving in protest is another last resort—do it only when all else fails.

Now, as for polling your fellow diners: Forget it. Democracy is a great way to elect congressmen, but it won't get you a steak cooked the way you want it. Also, it's *your* steak, which makes it *your* beef with the restaurant, not your fellow diners'. **If you want action, take action!** Take it to the higher-ups: the maître d', the manager, the owner if necessary. You'll be amazed how often they'll side with you against their own employees; after all, you're their bread and butter, the person who pays the bills. You'll get a new steak for your trouble, and positive reinforcement for yourself. (By the way, even though you had to fight for the right to a decent meal, don't neglect to leave a tip; but instead of putting it on the table, give it to the maître d' or manager on your way out. It adds a touch of class to your evening.)

The Magic of Self-Confidence

QUESTION 4: **The Tardy Date.**
Correct answer B

Sometimes, the best and only way to deal with a situation like this is to give the offender a taste of his own medicine. If you've expressed your irritation about your date's tardiness before, it's doubtful that your saying it again, under the same circumstances, will have much of an impact. More than likely, it will go in one ear and out the other. The one thing you don't want to do is create a pattern in which you tolerate another person's inconsiderate behavior at the expense of your own peace of mind. The more you allow others to take advantage of you, the farther off the track of the Circle you get. But, you might say to yourself, "Suppose, this time, my date has a legitimate reason for being late. I should wait to find out." Not good enough. We've all heard the story of the boy who cried wolf. How many times are you going to answer the call before you take a firm stand?

The only solution is to leave. It gets your message across and it gets results. It demonstrates your resolve and shows that your feelings should never be taken lightly. *That's* the pattern you want to create.

QUESTION 5: **The Movie Motor Mouths.**
Correct answer B

If people are bothering you, it's up to you to let them know it. There are two good reasons why you shouldn't leave the theatre and demand your money back: 1) you can't really expect the folks who run the theatre to be responsible for every loose set of vocal chords (unless the talkers are abusive—then you have a case for getting your money back) and 2) if you leave, you surrender your right to enjoy the movie—and, essentially, concede that others have the right to make you miserable. Your environment "punishes" or negatively reinforces you for your *un*self-confident act.

Now, as for calling an usher, you may want to do that eventually, but it's really more bother than necessary. You can take care of the problem with ease: All you have to do is make your presence felt, it's that simple. Glaring in a dark theatre, of course, is not going to get you very far, but a firm "shush" or "excuse me, could you take your talk into the lobby" will work wonders. **Peer pressure is a powerful tool: Know how to use it.** By asking the talkers to be quiet, you are speaking not only for yourself but for everyone around you. They'll appreciate that you've taken the initiative and made their movie-watching more enjoyable. They'll appreciate that you've championed their cause.

QUESTION 6: **The Boss's Party, in Sickness or in Health.**
Correct answer A

The most essential ingredient of self-confidence is your health. How can you expect to feel good about yourself if you don't feel well? Don't play games with your well-being, don't use it as a bargaining chip in your personal life or career. People who ignore this rule invariably pay the price later. Guard your health as one of your most valuable possessions—once you lose it, you can't go out and buy it back.

Going to a party, especially a party that you think might have some effect on your career, when you don't feel up to it just doesn't make sense. It's like betting you'll win a tennis match with your hands tied behind your back: You're giving yourself a handicap. If you think that going to the party in spite of how you feel will show the boss what you're made of, think again. Because when tomorrow comes, and you either call in sick or come to work sick after partying all evening, then the boss will *really* see what you're made of. And don't ask your boss how important it is that you go to the party; that's not the issue. The issue is how you feel. You don't have to prove anything to anyone; the decision is yours. Decline the invitation gracefully and go home to bed. *Now* the boss knows what you're made of. He knows you're secure enough in yourself to make a sound and sensible choice.

QUESTION 7: **Playing the Dating Game.**
Correct answer B

At first glance this question may seem designed for women only. Not true, certainly not today. The pressure to perform is something that makes everyone uncomfortable. Male or female, sometimes you just want to slow down and take it nice and easy. The only way to do that, if you want the relationship to continue to develop, is to explain exactly how you feel.

Giving in for the sake of the relationship is a contradiction in terms. What relationship? You're setting up a pattern—the classic one-sided arrangement—which, once set up, is next to impossible to change. By giving in you give up control. Compromising without conversation can't work either; one or both of you (probably both of you) will end up feeling unhappy and in most cases resentful. There's no reason to think your discomfort will subside—it may only get worse. You'll get in deeper than you'd planned.

The Self-Confidence Test

Making excuses is perhaps the easiest, but far from the best, solution. You're only postponing the decision. The situation, like a bad dream, will repeat itself over and over until you deal with it. After all, if you're serious about this relationship, how many times do you want to call off your dates at nine or ten in the evening?

Don't be swayed by circumstances; assert yourself over them. Make your feelings known; share them. They're as worthy of consideration as anyone else's.

QUESTION 8: **A Date with Destiny.**
Correct answer C

Unlike question 7, in this scenario talk can be more of an obstruction than an avenue of communication. It's difficult to put such feelings into words without their becoming confused and entangled—sometimes even lost. Words, in this case, tend to complicate rather than simplify. There is a natural tendency in all of us at moments like these to sound like politicians, not because we're trying to hide something, but because our feelings are so strong, words just won't do. They lessen the impact of the moment. **When talk is cheap, don't talk—act on your feelings.**

Sure, there is a risk of rejection here, but then **next to your health, the willingness to take risks is the main component of self-confidence.** Remember, a single *act* of self-confidence is the first step on the road to an enduring self-confidence. People who take risks (calculated risks, to be sure) are people who get what they're after. Be assertive in your affection, not aggressive; see how your partner responds. If you detect some holding back or discomfort, *then* talk it out. But there is a natural chem-

The Magic of Self-Confidence

istry at work here, and if you've gotten this far chances are your instincts are on target.

QUESTION 9: The Stereo Sales Pitch.
Correct answer C

Having self-confidence does not mean you are a know-it-all. It's knowing precisely what you *don't* know that counts, and being willing to seek the advice of people who *do* know. In fact, a good definition of a person with self-confidence is a person who knows how, when, and where to get the best available advice in matters outside his or her area of expertise. Nobody's an expert on everything: Don't buy the speakers until you're confident you're getting the best deal for the money.

Using technical terms and jargon is part of an old sales-pitch trick: It's a way of playing on the customer's insecurities. The salesperson is trying to manipulate you, to get you to pretend you know what he's talking about so you'll buy his merchandise. There's no need to prove yourself—you don't have to pretend. The people in this store are clearly not trying to help, they're trying to take advantage. Take your business elsewhere.

Don't buy your speakers until you've found a store where the salespeople talk in plain, simple English (you can find them, if you look hard enough). **Never settle for less than the best, even if it means asking for help.** If you have confidence in yourself, you're one tough customer.

The Self-Confidence Test

QUESTION 10: The Computer Curse.
Correct answer <u>A</u>

If you chose answer D, "curse the computer age," you're in good company. Cursing computers is a modern pastime; they are the great intimidators of the 1980s. But as good as it might make you feel to take a sledgehammer to one of these flashy silicon-chip monsters, it's not going to get you very far. Computers are here to stay, and the sooner you develop a working relationship with them, the sooner you'll be a giant step ahead of the crowd. I know: Only recently have I become comfortable sitting and working at a computer terminal, and it's true, computers do make some of life's less-than-pleasant chores easier. There's one more thing to keep in mind: It gives your confidence a lift to know you can do something well that most people can't even begin to do. You feel better prepared for the future than your neighbors. Think what it must have been like eighty years ago to be the only person on the block to own an automobile and know how to drive it. Working a computer can give you the same feeling of freedom and power.

Now, as to *how* to learn to use the computer: Again, if you want to know how to do something well, ask an expert. Efficiency is the key here; don't get bogged down and frustrated. If you do, you'll just be working against yourself.

You'll be surprised, if you ask the right people to help you, how much positive reinforcement you get, and how quickly you become an expert. Computers seem more formidable than they really are; their bark is worse than their bite. It's like learning how to drive a car: You might stall out a few times, but before long you begin to enjoy the new places you can go, the new roads you can travel.

The Magic of Self-Confidence

Take a computer for a spin around the block. Not only is it fun, but it gives you a big edge at work and at school.

QUESTION 11: The Idea Nobody Wanted.
Correct answer <u>C</u>

Rejection is a part of life—in fact, it's a very necessary and healthy part of life. It's what keeps us fresh, keeps us on our toes, keeps us from settling merely for the okay, and continuously striving for the very best. Ask any writer: Most have enough rejection slips to wallpaper their walls. The best writers are the ones who move on, who see in each rejection a challenge to overcome.

Winners are scrappy fighters. They have a knack for avoiding any lasting damage. Remember the little engine that could? You've got to keep on chugging along. Don't look back, don't waste precious time and energy rehashing what's already over and done. Whether your idea is wrong or the people who rejected it are, if it meets too much resistance then you have to accept that it's just not going to fly. Don't let the Circle of Self-Confidence come to a screeching halt over a single issue. Occasionally, the true act of self-confidence is well-considered, tactical *inaction*. Eventually people's attitudes may change and you might want to bring up your idea again, but for now go on to your next project.

Overcoming rejection is absolutely crucial to a successful career. If you want to win races, don't beat a dead horse—train new ones!

The Self-Confidence Test

QUESTION 12: Shortchanged.
Correct answer B

Never shortchange yourself. If you're angry and you're in the right—even if you have no way to prove it—don't try to shrug off your anger. That never works. Better you should get it off your chest: **Get angry at the people to blame, not at yourself for letting them get away with something.** You'll undoubtedly feel better after you've made your feelings known.

Writing an angry letter might give you a certain amount of personal satisfaction, but once it reaches the store it will probably go the way of the rotten fruit—into the dumpster. You have no guarantee that someone in authority will read it, or if someone does read it that it will make him stop and think. Your personal presence, your personal indignation, is powerful—probably more powerful than you realize. The pen may be mightier than the sword, but in cases like this, the sword gets quicker results. Even if you don't get your money back, you *will* get results: The people in the store will know you are a person who stands up for your rights and they won't let it happen again. You may not get your money back, but you will get respect!

Finally, there is a place for angry letters. If, after you have confronted the situation face to face, you want to pound your point home or get your feelings down on record, *then* write your letter.

QUESTION 13: Tomorrow on Your Mind.
Correct answer B

Your main concern here is that you know your stuff. That's all you *can* do, that's all you *want* to do. **Don't let**

The Magic of Self-Confidence

the event manipulate you; you are always in control. Going over your material again and again will only make you feel stale and maybe a little crazy (you already know what you're doing—why go around in circles, why punish yourself with dull repetition?). As for altering your schedule and going to bed early before you're tired, it will have the opposite effect from the one you hoped for. Rather than creating an environment conducive to rest, you will create a vacuum in which your anxiety level is almost sure to rise.

The best way to cope is to do something you enjoy, something to help you relax and take your mind off tomorrow. The fact is you're never going to feel perfectly at ease—and the moment you do, that's when you should begin to worry. Nervous energy serves an important purpose; it gives you an edge, a certain vitality and spark. Actors say that their best performances are always preceded by a good, healthy dose of stage fright; it indicates a build-up of adrenalin and positive energy. A little stage fright can do you a world of good, and more than likely will disappear the moment you walk out on to your own particular stage of action.

QUESTION 14: Excuses, Excuses.
Correct answer C

Never give up until you're good and ready to give up. **Persistence is a virtue—nine out of ten times it will pay off.** But coming straight to the point in an instance like this is not effective. It's bad policy to ask loaded questions of someone you hardly know. It turns people off, and it's too early in the game to start issuing ultimatums. You're acting defensively with no good reason to be

The Self-Confidence Test

defensive. Excuses, apologies—even outright refusals—are often more a question of timing than they are of feelings and desires.

Often, the best strategy is to change your strategy. Perhaps the person is shy, perhaps old-fashioned; perhaps—did you ever consider this?—the excuses for not seeing you were *not* excuses, but legitimate reasons. You just can't be sure. Instead of asking the person out to dinner, try something different. Suggest that you go for a walk together, that you go bowling or to the circus—anything! Maybe a lunch date will sound less threatening than a dinner date, and easier to say yes to. Before throwing in the towel, you have to take into account the person's idiosyncrasies and biases. And after all, there's nothing wrong with lunch: It's the same thing as dinner, only a few hours earlier. Also, lunch has a way of leading to dinner, dinner to drinks, and so on.

QUESTION 15: **Romance Interruptus.**
Correct answer B

First off, you didn't do anything wrong! That's the number-one thing to keep in mind. The danger here is that you come down so hard on yourself that you lose sight of the real problem—a problem that, if you look at the situation objectively for a moment, you'll see rests on the other side of the relationship. *You* have not changed, *you* are not to blame.

You might conclude that you can live without all the aggravation; but, the truth be known, it's much more aggravating to write off a relationship without knowing why you have to do so. You owe it to yourself to get to the bottom of the trouble. Waiting for the other person to

The Magic of Self-Confidence

come around won't get you there—but it will get you a roller-coaster ride of expectation and disappointment.

Where you have made an emotional investment, you have a right to expect direct, straightforward answers. Don't stop until you get them. For all you know, the problem has nothing to do with you (a death in the family, for instance). Or perhaps it has something to do with the relationship itself; perhaps the other person has been hurt before and doesn't want to get hurt again. It could be anything, and if you feel strongly enough about the relationship, find out the answers. **You can't begin to deal with someone or something until you know who or what you're dealing with.**

Ten-Point Bonus Question:

QUESTION 16: **Road to Responsibility.**
Correct answer B

Admitting your own mistakes is a good idea. Let's call it enlightened self-interest. By taking the blame, by owning up to your errors straightaway, you turn a potential negative into a definite positive. You take the wind out of your competitors' sails. You show people how secure you are in yourself—that you have nothing to hide from them. And, perhaps most important, you indicate how unusual and special you are.

Taking responsibility for your actions (not only the blame, but also the credit when it is due you) is a mark of distinction and strength. I can think of no more convincing or powerful argument for trusting someone than that he or she is willing to face up to imperfection. This is probably the easiest question in the quiz to answer correctly and the hardest to put into practice. **If you have**

The Self-Confidence Test

the confidence to accept failure, there is absolutely no doubt that you have the confidence to achieve success.

Scoring

For every correct answer to questions 1 through 15, score six points. A correct answer to number 16 is worth ten bonus points.

0–20

Self-awareness, sensitivity, and honesty are your strong points. You are a SEEKER, a person open to change who lacks only a clear sense of purpose. You are like a well-qualified job applicant who doesn't know the mechanics of writing a résumé. This book will help you bring your desires and aspirations into focus.

21–50

Most people who take the test score in this range. You are the STRIVER, the MOVER. Self-confidence and self-doubt, success and disappointment, strength of purpose and fear of failure—you experience all of these feelings in your drive to achieve your goals. There are areas of your life you feel good about, and others that you feel leave room for improvement. Self-confidence is within your grasp. As you read on you will learn more about how to take hold and make use of it in specific situations.

51–80

You are a SELF-STARTER. You know what you want and you're ready to go out and get it. You feel good about yourself, but there remains a nagging sense of dissatisfaction. This book will give you the support and guidance you need to give you the edge, to take you that final step.

81–100

The Circle of Self-Confidence is already in motion. With this book at your side, you'll keep it oiled and running smoothly in every situation.

4
Going the Distance

*F*or thousands of years, from the Olympic Games of ancient Greece to the glory days of Babe Ruth and Jesse Owens to the present-day era of sports heroes and heroines, athletes have played a unique and very special role in society. They thrive on competition. It is their lifeblood, their reason for being. To succeed, they must meet and overcome new challenges every day. They define for us qualities of mental and physical toughness, of individual character and of team effort, endurance, perseverance, and resilience. We find in their personal and ongoing battles clear-cut and exaggerated versions of our own. By the nature of the roles they play, athletes are the chief practitioners of the magic of self-confidence.

Even if you don't participate in athletics, your suc-

The Magic of Self-Confidence

cesses and failures in other areas of life are often measured and described by what I call, for lack of a better term, *jockese*. "The ball is in your court," someone might say if it's up to you to make the next move, or "take the ball and run with it" if you're given an opportunity to prove your skills. Some guys claim they've "scored" with a date when they don't want to admit that they just plain "struck out." Everyone likes to "score points" with the boss, but no one wants to get "thrown for a loss." We all have "hurdles" to get over but it's worth it if we make it into "the winner's circle." And no matter what you're trying to accomplish in life—whether it be a successful marriage, business, or career—you have to be willing to "go the distance."

What makes the athlete run? How does the marathoner maintain the will to win in the face of physical and emotional exhaustion? What induces the tennis player to go back out on the court after a devastating and heartbreaking loss? What drives the sprinter, the swimmer, indeed any athlete to the outer limit of his or her ability? The answers to these questions will help us understand where self-confidence comes from and what it can do. In this chapter we will explore the athlete's will to win, and how you can apply the principles to your own life. The material is drawn from various sources, including personal interviews with sports figures.

* * *

Gayle Olinekova is a physical-finess legend. She is a world-class marathon runner, body-builder, cyclist, and speed skater. *Sports Illustrated,* in an outstanding feature article, said she has "the greatest legs ever to stride the earth." Her physique is extraordinary—powerful but perfectly proportioned. To her, physical fitness is an artistic endeavor, and if the shape she's in is any indication, she has reached the pinnacle of her craft.

She is the author of two books, *Go For It!* and *Legs!* and runs a successful health and fitness spa in St. Croix, Virgin Islands. She has never stopped pushing herself. She has always sought out new ambitions to realize, new heights to climb.

"Sure," Gayle said when asked if there are moments when she's down on herself, when she feels she can't go on, "there have been setbacks, too many times to count. There have been times when I've begun to feel sorry for myself—once, for instance, when I was on crutches for six months. But you have to keep such things in perspective. My problems—most people's problems—are no bigger than ripples in the ocean. In time, they vanish. You have to laugh at yourself, it does you a world of good. Not only that," she added, "but it's great for the stomach muscles as well.

"I received a letter recently," she went on, "from a man who entered the wheelchair division of the Boston Marathon. He said *I* inspired *him*. But when I'm running twenty miles, and my legs begin to ache, I think of him. I think of how exceptional an individual he must be, and of how lucky I am. You see, I can feel the ache in my legs, which is something many people are not fortunate enough to feel. The man in the wheelchair, he is the *true* inspiration."

Perspective. Always keep your problems in perspective. Small setbacks, if you allow them to, can gnaw away at your confidence like parasites—and the more energy you expend worrying about them, the more nourishment you give them. Instead of maintaining the Circle's momentum, you risk spinning dizzily out of control. In sports as in every enterprise, failure and disappointment are facts of life. Don't let them get the best of you. Do you remember the wizard in the movie *The Wizard of Oz*—the fiery and terrible tyrant who turns out to be a mere fabrication of the tiny and sheepish man in the booth? *That's* the difference between how you perceive your failures and what they really amount to. It's up to you: a tidal wave of your own making, or a tiny, vanishing ripple in the ocean.

"When I'm down," Gayle continued, "I don't sit around and meditate, and I don't wait for someone else to come and give me a pep talk. I go out and have a fast and furious workout!"

Gayle believes we are all born with the will to survive, which is just another way of saying the will to succeed. She says it's like "a flame burning within. We have the choice either to accept or deny it. The key is whether or not we nurture that flame.

"Put all your effort into coordinating mind and body to achieve your goals; self-respect, self-esteem, the quiet power of self-confidence will naturally follow."

The essence of success, she told me, is preparation. "When I run a marathon, the real work comes *before* I step up to the starting line. Winning depends on the investment you are willing to make; I have a responsibility to myself to do the very best I possibly can. Otherwise, I wouldn't be standing on the starting line.

"All my life," Gayle concluded, "I've believed that dreams come true. I've been accused of being a dreamer, but that's what keeps me going, keeps me striving. I want, more than anything, to realize my dreams. It's not always easy to follow your heart, but I know if I do, I will succeed."

* * *

Going the Distance

Over the past ten years Chris Evert Lloyd has dominated women's tennis. She is a patient, precision player who wears down opponents with her firm, deep ground strokes and her cool under pressure. As anyone who follows her game and her career knows, she is more than a tennis player of exquisite skill, she is a champion with class, gracious both in victory and defeat. On the court and off she is composed, disciplined and always in control.

Perhaps most remarkable about Chris Evert Lloyd is that over the years she has overcome disillusionment, personal pain, and long periods of self-doubt to achieve her tenacious, determined, and unaffected appearance. "Before a match, I want to block out all distractions; if the mind is strong, you can do anything. It's a form of hypnotism. You've got to take the initiative and play *your* game. In a decisive set, confidence is the difference," she wrote in her autobiography, *Chrissie: My Own Story*.

Concentrating on the task at hand can make the difference between attaining your goal and falling short. As Chris points out, it is a form of self-hypnosis—a state of mind worth rehearsing. There are any number of ways to do this. In a physical conditioning program, for instance, whether it be running, dancing, tennis, or your favorite sport, concentrate all your energy on your body and muscles—how they respond, how they work, how to make them excel. A mental exercise might be to read for an hour without lifting your eyes from the page—lose yourself in the words and the story. It may be tough at first, but with practice you'll find concentration enhances the pleasure of the activity.

Concentration is only half the story, however. Relaxation—allowing your mind the freedom to wander—is

The Magic of Self-Confidence

just as important. "Whether it's dinner, dancing, music, or a massage," Chris says, "you need a few diversions that completely remove you from the pressures of your profession."

Focus all your energies, the way a magnifying glass focuses light, on your object. What causes many people to fail is in fact their *fear* of failure—it breaks their concentration, and they lose their edge. Focus instead on completing and preserving the Circle.

Chris Evert Lloyd was, by her own admission, shy and insecure when she was young. But she left those insecurities behind to become a champion. She attributes her success to "mental strength, belief in myself, guts and the ability never to give up. I never looked back, never dwelled on my defeats. I always looked ahead."

Patience and precision—they are the qualities of sound mental conditioning that power the winning stroke.

* * *

How far can a man fly on his own, unaided by machine or mechanical device? That's the question track star Carl Lewis is determined to answer. He dreams of leaping farther than any other human being ever has—and it's a goal well within his reach. Fifteen years ago Bob Beamon set the world record for the long jump: 29 feet, 2½ inches. At this writing, Carl Lewis has jumped 28 feet, 9 inches, just 5½ inches off the record. No one else competing in the long jump today comes close; Carl Lewis's only competition is himself. Every time he jumps, he is striving to outdo himself. (Incidentally, Carl Lewis is also the third-fastest man in the world: He's run the 100 meters in ten seconds flat, five hundredths of a second off the world record.) Lewis' quote came from the article by

Going the Distance

Charles Siebert in *Esquire* magazine's April, 1983 issue.

In high school, Carl Lewis was not an outstanding track and field competitor. "I was an average township athlete, small and slow. Simple." He worked long and hard for every inch and every second. Through sheer determination, he pushed himself to greatness. In the 1980 Olympic trials, he competed in both the long jump and the 100 meters, finishing first and fourth respectively. "That was expected, but I was disappointed. People told me, 'That's because you're going for the double.' But it was a good disappointment because everyone was telling me I couldn't do both and I hate being told I can't do something. I can't take it."

Carl Lewis is the consummate athlete. As an amateur, he is unpaid; he runs and he jumps simply for the thrill of it. His commitment is absolute: "I am only really comfortable when I run or when I sleep. The rest of the time I just complain." He exemplifies the power of individual will, effort, and desire. Lewis shows by his accomplishments that there is no ambition too high to strive for. If you want to fly, you can; you can fly on the wings of total commitment and unyielding purpose. You owe it to yourself to try.

"The records are in Carl Lewis," he reflects. "Getting them is just part of finding out who he is. If I don't, it will be a flat waste of person."

* * *

So, what makes the great athletes great? What makes them run, what makes them win? The obvious answer is physical ability, but clearly that alone is not enough. There is something more, something extra that ignites a man or woman to exploit that physical ability and stretch it to the limit. If we consider these three biographical sketches, I think we'll find several common threads. Let's tie them together.

Self-awareness. The great athletes know exactly what they want; their goals are clearly defined. They know their strengths and weaknesses, and consequently can emphasize their strengths and de-emphasize their weaknesses.

Self-control. They are disciplined and extremely hard workers—dedicated to their tasks. They are self-interested in the best sense of the word: They take care of themselves.

Courage. They are unafraid of failure. They don't enjoy defeat, but they don't shy away from the possibility of it. They see defeat as a temporary—and correctable—condition.

The ability to dream. The great athletes' only limitations are those they set for themselves. They think big and defy limitations. If a goal is conceivable, they believe they are capable of achieving it.

These are the characteristics of those people we call "success stories." They have that spark of self-confidence that enables them to go the distance.

5

The Art of Self-Confidence, the Business of Success

*J*ack Hilton is an innovator, a pioneer in the field of television and corporate communications. He embodies the entrepreneurial spirit of the 1980s. A century ago that spirit belonged to the pioneers of the oil, steel, and automobile industries. They created new technologies and built empires. Today, when those industrial empires—Exxon, Ford Motor Company, Union Carbide, and many others—turn to the latest and most powerful technology, telecommunications, they turn to Jack Hilton.

Jack Hilton Incorporated prepares corporate executives, politicians, and television personalities for the challenges of television exposure. How to handle harsh questions and the harsh lights; how to make a point and make it well; how to do battle, on an equal footing, with

The Magic of Self-Confidence

the Mike Wallaces and Phil Donahues of the world—how to present themselves with confidence. To judge by his list of clients—some 300 of the Fortune 500 companies and nearly 500 politicians on both the local and national level—the business Jack Hilton conceived, designed, and built in ten short years has brought him a large measure of success.

Success seems to follow wherever Jack Hilton goes. He is the author of two books,* a developer and producer of television programs, a specialist in corporate video-conferencing, and, for the 1984 presidential campaign, a special correspondent and commentator for CBS News. He is a high-powered man sitting smack in the middle of a vibrant, high-powered, very successful business, which may explain why, when I first entered his midtown Manhattan office, I was (pleasantly) surprised to find him casually dressed in a green crew-neck sweater, grey corduroy slacks, and moccasins. Not a pin stripe or cuff link in sight.

Hilton is a tall, ruggedly good-looking man, smooth, extroverted, and assertive—comfortably self-assured. His easygoing manner and dress say a great deal about the man and his sensibilities: If you've got it, no need to flaunt it. (Image is a recurring theme in *The Magic of Self-Confidence.* Remember that the image you cultivate has a significant bearing on how others respond to you.) At 46, Jack Hilton is exactly where he wants to be, doing exactly what he wants to do. He appears as close to contentment as any man of energy and ambition can be. How did it come about? How did he get here?

"Frankly," he said, "I think I've made the right

The TV Inquisitors (Chamberlain International Publishers) and *On Television: A Survival Guide for Media Interviews* (AMACOM)

choices—and even more important, once I've made a decision, I've always followed through. In business and the professions, once you make a decision, you have to act on it. The decision you make right now, no matter how difficult, will only become *more* difficult to make as time passes."

Jack Hilton has made a career out of changing directions—changing directions in all the right ways. He is a man who constantly re-evaluates, who sorts out his options, decides what he wants, then makes his move. He has never shied away from the risks and uncertainties of change.

He began his career on the air, in front of the cameras, at WGN-TV in Chicago, and eventually moved into a position of greater control, behind the cameras in production. Hilton soon found himself growing increasingly restless in television, and thought his talents might be better served and less confined elsewhere. He was struck by the greater array of options, opportunities, and challenges offered by a career in business.

"In my early thirties," he said, "I decided I had better change directions fast, or I might never again get the chance."

He sought out the most advantageous way to make a smooth transition from the world of the media to the world of business, and found it at the J. Walter Thompson advertising agency. The move paid off like a long shot. By the age of thirty-six, he was named president of the ad agency's telecommunications division—and in his case it was not a matter of luck. Hilton had carefully hedged his bets: When he made the move into business he did not go into banking, heavy industry, transportation, or real estate—he went in the direction his knowledge, expertise, and interest led him.

The Magic of Self-Confidence

Even as he rose to a position of prominence at J. Walter Thompson, Hilton continued to shuffle the deck and deal himself new cards. He had what he calls now "a pipe dream." "I always aspired," he said, "as I think most people do, to run my own shop. I wanted autonomy—the biggest challenge of all when you get down to it . . . no one to blame but yourself if things don't work out.

"It occurred to me that here I was with an insight into television and the press and how they work, and in close personal proximity to a number of heavy breathers in American business. I gained an appreciation for them and how they operated. I saw for myself their apprehension—hatred, anger, fear, call it what you will—of the media. I thought perhaps it would be useful, and profitable as well, to construct a bridge between these two worlds. Jack Hilton Inc. came about as a result of my parallel, but different, personal and professional experiences."

Today some of the most powerful and influential people in America pay him well, and gladly, to use the bridge he has built. I asked if he ever experiences doubt; if, even in the face of his obvious success, he ever steps back and questions whether he had made the right moves, whether he is heading in the right direction.

"Oh, sure, every step of the way. There have always been low points, the anguish and second-guessing, and there always will be. . . . But it's in my nature to be persistent—perhaps 'stubborn' is a better word. I don't give up easily."

When asked if he has any advice to offer someone who wants to make the most out of a career in business, he paused and took a stab at it:

"You have to invest yourself. There are no nine-to-five possibilities in terms of true success in business or the professions. Dedication is the key. I regard myself as a

The Art of Self-Confidence, the Business of Success

fairly intelligent person and, now, as a fairly experienced person—but I don't know that I am such a whiz-bang in terms of I.Q. I'm not sure I can always outthink you, but I can usually outwork you. That often results in the *appearance* that I can outthink you.

"The first step," he went on, "whenever you face a career move, decision, or whatever, is to make an honest assessment of yourself: What are your strengths and weaknesses? What experience do you have? What opportunities do you foresee? *Maximize your strengths.* Learn as much as you possibly can about your area of interest or expertise. Make yourself a specialist, make yourself valuable to others.

"I regard what I do professionally as something I do twenty-four hours a day, seven days a week. It's not that I'm a workaholic, although some might say so. It's just that my *vocation* is also my *avocation.*"

The secret of Jack Hilton's success is his relationship to his work. He chose to do with his life something he takes pleasure in doing. The choices he has made have been the right choices because they have been determined not by circumstances or by default, but by his own hopes, dreams, and desires. In this way he is like an artist, his work an integral part of his life, a labor of love. If you perceive your work as no more than a necessary nine-to-five evil, then that's what it will always be. Time will become your taskmaster, and your job an alien and oppressive force. Consider changing jobs, changing directions, changing your life. And if that sounds like too tall an order, remember the little engine that could! A career should be measured not on a time clock but on a lifelong calendar. Success is built not around coffee breaks and lunch hours, but upon a lifetime of rewarding work well done.

The Magic of Self-Confidence

We know that the image you project has a significant impact on how people respond to you—and thus on how you feel about yourself and on what you do or don't accomplish. Jack Hilton is in the business of enhancing image and building confidence, of teaching people how to handle themselves in difficult public situations. Here are some of his tips for preparing his clients for job interviews, oral presentations or examinations, and in fact for almost any social situation.

PREPARATION

"The key to everything we do here," he said, "is embodied in the word *preparation*. When you see someone in a position of prominence on television, and he or she seems self-assured, seems to speak off the cuff, with great eloquence and command, that person, in all likelihood, is about as spontaneous as a performance by the Joffrey Ballet. It's that carefully diagrammed, constructed, and rehearsed.

Whenever you approach a social or public situation whose outcome is important to you, always think through the circumstances in advance.

- Decide what you want to accomplish and how you will do so.
- Consider the other people involved: How will they respond? What will they do, what will they say, what will they want from you?
- Talk the matter through with a friend, even try role-playing if you feel it will help.

Your best defense against nerves is meticulous preparation and rehearsal. You can't have ballet without choreography.

The Art of Self-Confidence, the Business of Success

THE EVENT ITSELF

Now, the moment you've been preparing for is here. What can you do—physically and strategically—to make the kind of statement about yourself that you want to make? The place to start, says Hilton, is with body language (he tests his clients on videotape, but suggests that a mirror will suffice):

- Make eye contact frequently.
- Lean forward, never backward; don't crouch.
- Be animated; gesture with your hands.
- Speak clearly and deliberately.

Finally, here are some ways to win people over:

- Be enthusiastic about what you have to say.
- Be a good listener, respond to the people around you.
- Be open and accessible; don't be afraid of injecting personal anecdotes into a conversation.
- Be cool; maintain your composure.

The idea here—from rehearsal to performance—is to create and project an *image* of self-confidence. "The successful person in business," said Hilton, "indeed, any successful individual, is, in some sense, an actor."

Edwin Newman, the NBC newsman, once said about stage fright and nervous energy: "The only difference between the pros and the novices is that the pros have trained the butterflies to fly in formation."

Success comes not from fearlessness, but from the *art* of self-control.

6

For Women Only. Mouseburger and Miss America: Models of Self-Confidence

"Some days," says Helen Gurley Brown, "I feel genuine *power* in my hands and it feels good."

For someone who describes herself as a "mouseburger," Helen Gurley Brown knows a lot about power and influence—about how to acquire them and how to put them to use. Her impact on today's generation of women is widely felt, and her disciples are everywhere: in boardrooms and bedrooms, in marriages and movies.

With the publication in the early '60s of her book *Sex and the Single Girl*, she revolutionized the way America looked at its young women—and the way America's young women looked at *themselves*. Young unmarried females, it turned out, were not as innocent and pure as we were led to believe; in fact—and this was what hit

The Magic of Self-Confidence

home—young unmarried females had many of the same urges and desires that young unmarried *males* had. In the home, in the office, and in love, the career girl wanted her piece of the pie, too.

Helen Gurley Brown opened doors and minds that had long been shut tight. A revolutionary in the sexual revolution, a liberator in the women's movement, she didn't take off her bra and burn it in the streets, but instead took off society's prejudices and hangups and burned them in print. For twenty-five years she has been a champion of equal rights and equal opportunity for women. She has provided women with the encouragement, the guidance, and the opportunity to explore parts of themselves—sexually, emotionally, and intellectually—that had previously been in limbo, in the forbidden zone. She tore down the "Do Not Enter" signs, and put out the welcome mat.

The power Helen Gurley Brown holds in her hands is reflected in her divers accomplishments. She is the author of a second best-selling book, *Having It All*, she is a well-known television personality, and she has been married for twenty-five years to David Brown, co-producer of such films as *Jaws*, *The Sting*, and *The Verdict*. The most striking testament to her influence, however, is that she is the creator of, and the force behind, *Cosmopolitan* magazine as we know it today.

She has been *Cosmo*'s editor for over twenty years, and in that time has shaped the magazine in her own image. Its commitment to the ideal of feminine self-reliance and its self-help credo have been a touchstone to its readers around the world. *Cosmo* has been a banner leading women into the battles of everyday life, urging them onward and upward in business affairs and in affairs of the heart. Helen Gurley Brown is a trailblazer, a success in love, in business, and in self-expression. Whatever self-confidence is, she has it; wherever it comes from, she's been there and back. She nurtured and used it masterfully to carve out of her environment, if not a small empire, then certainly the kind of home, career, and influence many of us aspire to. Like Julius Caesar, she came, she saw, she conquered.

But what, you might legitimately ask yourself, does Helen Gurley Brown have to offer *you*? Isn't she in a different league? Doesn't she live and work on an entirely different stratum of society, separated from most of us by an accident of fate, by the advantages of her wealth and position? The question is: Was she dealt a royal flush, like Prince Charles or Princess Caroline or the Kennedys, or does she just play a great game? A quick look at her background gives us the answer:

She spent what she calls her "problem-ripe" youth in Arkansas, in Little Rock and a couple of small Ozark Mountain towns that, in the 1930s, were about as far away as you could get, in spirit and in temperament, from Los Angeles or New York. In other words, she was not born to the kind of power she would one day acquire; in fact, she was born nowhere near it. Like millions of other young, supposedly innocent and unquestionably frightened Americans, she packed up her hopes and dreams and headed west, seeking her fame and fortune. First stop on a long trip: a $6-a-week job as a secretary at an L.A. radio station. A succession of seventeen—seventeen!—secretarial jobs followed, and a second big move, this time east, to New York. Finally, after learning the ropes from the bottom up and the inside out, she squeezed into a position as a copywriter at an ad agency. She climbed the ladder one slippery rung at a time. At nights and on weekends, she drew on her experiences and adventures as a single girl in New York to write a book—and the rest is history.

Success didn't come looking for Helen Gurley Brown. She went out and found it. She took hold and hasn't let go since. She developed her own greatest assets: a certain street smarts and savvy, the sheer determination to do well, and an incurable desire to succeed. She has played her cards well, with patience, persistence, and pluck.

When I asked her the secret of having it all, she didn't pause a moment: "It's like that John Houseman commercial: You have to do it the old-fashioned way, you have to earn it. . . . You have to be hungry."

Helen Gurley Brown is proud of her roots as a "mouseburger," and through it all, she says, continues to be one. Her experience speaks directly to the mouseburger. So, just exactly what *is* a "mouseburger"? As described in *Having It All*, she is a women who must come from behind, who must start at the bottom to get to the top. She was born neither rich nor gorgeous, she does not have a Ph.D. from M.I.T. and has absolutely no intention of getting one. She knows what it means to struggle, has a pretty good idea of what she wants, but isn't quite sure how to get it. She's not afraid to scratch and claw, if that's what it takes, and she won't back away from a challenge. Meeting and mating men is very likely an area of great anxiety for her—but she'd sooner give up life than give up the opportunity to feel that anxiety.

"Of course you're scared," Helen says. "Of course you sometimes feel like a schlep. There's a vulnerability in all of us; you never lose it, and that's fine." The feeling of inadequacy, of not being "good enough," she says, is something most women experience. "But you have to get your foot in the door, give your potentialities the chance to develop. And at least half of what you do is bound to be unpleasant. What's most important, what's most challenging, is that you get through the day-to-day drudgery. You don't have to take chances, you don't have to burn the bridges behind you. You have only to dare to do the dirty work, and to seize opportunity when it comes. There's no way you can succeed and have the lovely spoils—money, recognition, deep satisfaction—unless you're willing to put in the hours.

"You gain confidence," she went on, "by figuring out what it is you do well, and doing it for a long time. Whether you're good on the racquetball court or good in bed, that's what gets you through. When I was a young single girl, just getting started, there was one thing I knew I could do well: I knew I could bring *any* man to orgasm. It was an area of expertise that sustained me through rough times, through the loss of jobs and through heartbreak."

Everyone hurts, everyone suffers, everyone has dark and dangerous hours of gloom and doom. "But you don't have to jump off a roof," she says. Knowing what you do well and keeping it in mind, then drawing on it in times of pain and doubt, is like taking a warm, relaxing bath. It soothes the hurt, it gets you through the night.

Ms. Brown urges women to go out into the workplace, choose a career and follow it. A career, she says, can do wonders for your marriage, for your sexuality, for yourself—not to mention, for your wallet. "Nothing is as much *fun* as achieving."

Her message is simply: Don't waste. Use what you have, and take what is offered. Whatever you do, do it with a *passion*. Work hard, love hard, live hard. She is committed to living a full, thick, lush life. Her self-confidence comes, to turn a phrase, from confiding in herself, from believing in her ability, her strength, and

The Magic of Self-Confidence

her power, and from not giving up, in the best *and* worst of times.

Here is a small sampling of the wit and wisdom from her book, *Having It All:*

On exercise:
"Something you can do with relative simplicity in order to have control over your life, to change it for the better."

On sexuality:
"Sexual means loving your body, loving being a woman, loving *men*, loving *their* bodies and loving your bodies together."

On men:
"Just because men are frequently irresponsible and behave detestably does not mean they cannot love deeply."

On love:
"Love doesn't drop on you unexpectedly; you have to give off signals, sort of like an amateur radio operator."

On marriage:
"Balancing is what a marriage is . . . balancing your needs against his and trying to see that both sides get taken care of."

On career:
"Work at the job you're *in*. Do more than your share in that job. Study. Inch along. Pile up 'goodness' until you are *so* good everybody can see it and not ignore you."

Now let's turn from the power behind *Cosmopolitan* to the power in front of it. Pick up a copy and look at the cover. What do you see? You see a woman who is not afraid to look you straight in the eye, who carries herself with poise and sophistication, who is sexy, self-assured, and, chances are, successful. You see, in short, the image of the woman Helen Gurley Brown urges *you* to be—a woman whose motto could very well be "having it all." The power behind *Cosmo* is reflected on its cover. Its substance *is* its style.

Style, says Webster, is "the way in which anything is made or done"; but the dictionary doesn't stop there, it also defines style as "distinction, excellence, originality and character in any form of artistic expression." Now, all of us have *a* style (the first definition); the key is to have *style* (second definition), to have the distinction and character to look the world straight in the eye and meet it on *your* terms.

Which brings us to Kylene Barker. *Style* has been Kylene's watchword. In fact, she's made a career out of it. Looking back, she traces the origin of that career to a day in the fourth grade. She and her family, like much of the country, were watching the Miss America pageant on television. And like many other girls her age, Kylene decided that day that *she* wanted to become Miss America. "The winner," she told me, "did a wonderful trampoline act in the talent competition. She inspired me. I already loved gymnastics, and she gave me the incentive to spend even more time in the gym and to spend it well. Growing up, I tended to be very competitive—and I knew the rewards wouldn't come easy, that I'd have to work hard for them."

In 1979 her determination and competitive spirit brought her to the place she'd always dreamed of: Atlantic City, where she represented her home state of Virginia in *the* contest. After a smashing gymnastics routine

The Magic of Self-Confidence

that brought the house down, Kylene Barker was crowned Miss America, 1979. She recalls the night before:

"I learned from gymnastics that the only way to get a routine down is to go over every move again and again and again until you feel perfectly comfortable doing it. That's what I did that night, in my head: I watched myself, over and over, walking down the runway, crowned and victorious, until it seemed perfectly natural and comfortable. From gymnastics I acquired the habit of rehearsal, and now—as on that night in Atlantic City—before I do anything important, I go over every move, very carefully, in my head. I call it 'making pictures.' Picture," she said, "a little video machine in my mind's eye that I can run forward and back. I even use it afterward to analyze, a kind of instant replay."

Today, Kylene is the owner of a thriving designer-clothes boutique, d. Kylene, on fashionable Worth Avenue in Palm Beach, Florida. She is the co-author of the recently published book *Southern Beauty*, which tells the story of the path she followed to Atlantic City, and also offers valuable advice on fitness, beauty, and fashion. She has gone on tour across the country for Clairol, has put together an exercise album, and has made frequent appearances on the fashion segment of "The Today Show" on NBC. "I feel good about my career," she says, "and I feel it's rounding into shape. I've known what I wanted and I've wasted as little time as possible to get it." Ever since the fourth grade, when she first imagined herself as Miss America, she has been "making pictures" and making them come true. Kylene has warmth, charm and, as the title of her book says, southern beauty. In a word, she has *style*.

"Looking your best does it," she told me. "It does

wonders for your self-esteem and self-confidence. Take care of yourself, polish yourself, stay fit, work on your hair style, your hair color, your makeup; choose the clothes you wear carefully. The trick is to have the stamina and presence to *look* cool, confident, and comfortable."

Look back now at the cover of *Cosmopolitan*. What you see there is a *model* of self-confidence—and this perception comes strictly from the way she *looks* (you know nothing else about her). You can bet your bottom dollar that she has worked very hard to get that look, and works very hard to keep it. What many of us tend to forget is that we have control over our appearance. Think of yourself as a painter and your body as the canvas: You choose the color, you choose the shape, you choose the *style*. If you want to lose weight, eat less; if you want to improve your shape, exercise more; if you want to feel more sexy, wear something sexy.

Of course, easier said than done. But you don't have to go it alone. From *Short Chic* to *Color Me Beautiful* to *Jane Fonda's Workout Book*, the bookstores are bursting at the seams with diet, exercise, fashion, fitness, and makeup books waiting for you to find them. There's sure to be something that speaks to your needs and desires, and many of the books are available in libraries as well.

Psychologically, though, it might be worth it to pay the price of the book. The book is yours, you paid for it, it gives you one more incentive to follow through. Finally, the bottom line is how much you *want* to improve your appearance. It comes down to desire. If you feel you are overweight, for instance, you have to hunger more for the feeling of sexiness and success than you hunger for dessert. You can do it with or without the books, but you have to *do it*.

The Magic of Self-Confidence

"The way you look," says Kylene, "has an extraordinary effect on how you feel, how you feel about yourself, and how others feel about *you.*" *Style,* says Webster, is an "artistic expression." It is a reflection of how much you care about yourself. If you care about yourself enough to look sexy and self-assured, then, over time, you will. *That* is the beauty of self-confidence.

7
Life's Scenarios

I'd like to introduce you to Molly and Sam. They're going to help us clear up some common problems and answer some tough questions. We'll run them through a few mazes (mazes that may seem very familiar to you) and see where they come out.

Sam is a bright guy, fun at a party, and if things go right for him, he could go far. But he has some nagging doubts—in fact, he has plenty. He's experienced personal and professional disappointments, and he wonders sometimes why his life doesn't run more smoothly. He's worried about the future and about making the wrong moves.

Molly is smart and sensitive with a lot on the ball. She's career oriented and she has ambitious plans for herself. There are moments, however, when the obstacles in her path seem steep and she questions whether she can overcome them. Furthermore, she knows she could stand to lose a few pounds, but she's looking for the diet and exercise plan that's right for her. She's not crazy about the guys who ask her out, and she tends to be anxious about dating in general (as, in fact, is Sam, but he would less readily admit it).

Eight short scenarios, featuring our two new friends, follow. They are situations in which you may have found yourself in the past and will probably find yourself in the future. This chapter is like that old game "What's wrong in this picture?" While you read, ask yourself what Molly and Sam are doing right and what they are doing wrong. Examine each action they take and decide whether or not it's likely to elicit a response of positive reinforcement. Where is the Circle of Self-Confidence running smoothly, and where is it in need of repair? Don't be any easier on Molly and Sam than you would be on yourself.

Following each scenario is a complete analysis, a step-by-step guide with specific suggestions to help *you* confront similar situations.

Life's Scenarios

Scenario #1: **The Test**

Sam's nerves are on edge; he's not exactly scared, but he's feeling tense and uneasy. He has spent weeks preparing for tomorrow's big test, the big presentation, and now that it's just around the corner he suddenly realizes it's absolutely crucial that he outperform everyone else. He decides that tomorrow he must prove himself, that this test will either make him or break him. He's restless, he can't sit still. He glances over his notes but can't concentrate. He turns on the TV and turns it off; he paces up and down like a caged animal. He considers going to bed early but knows he's not even tired. Instead, he organizes everything he'll need for tomorrow, puts it all in one place, and heads out for a long brisk walk.

The next morning, having set his alarm for six o'clock rather than seven to ensure that he doesn't oversleep, Sam rises an hour earlier than usual. Consequently, he reaches the appointed place with plenty of time to spare—in fact, he's the first to arrive. He takes a seat and waits, watching his peers and inquisitors file in. The test begins.

Sam does well. There are a few shaky moments, but all in all, he makes the points he wanted to make. Still, he's not satisfied, and he spends the afternoon berating himself and complaining to his friends about how he blew it.

ANALYSIS

Sam's instincts are right on the mark here; his attitudes, however, seem designed to undermine him. He's prepared and he's organized—and **preparation and organization are essential prerequisites to taking a test or giving a presentation.** Never wait until the last minute. Always remember the universal law: "The last minute shall invariably cometh and goeth quicker than you

The Magic of Self-Confidence

thought it would." There's no rule that says you can't start getting ready for a test months ahead of time.

Sam is also right to leave the house; there's no point in poring any longer over his notes. Getting out of his cage for a few hours will clear his mind, give him some room to breathe. His nervous energy is a good sign as well; it shows he's not taking tomorrow too lightly (there's a big difference between *self*-confidence and *over*confidence). But he goes too far: By telling himself that this is the test that will make or break him, he heaps unnecessary—and often destructive—pressure upon himself. I had a friend in college who had the same problem. Every single test was a proving ground for him, a measure of his own self-worth. It drove him up a wall, and consequently, when test time came, he froze; he had created an obstacle within himself too great to overcome. He did the intelligent thing though: On the day of the test he sought out the professor and explained his problem. The professor allowed him to retake the test later under more comfortable circumstances. Most people will go out of their way to give you a second chance; actual make-it-or-break-it situations are extremely rare.

The next morning, Sam is only feeding his anxiety by getting up an hour earlier than necessary. Not only is he losing a precious hour of sleep, but he's giving himself that much more time to fret. Never arrive at a test more than a few minutes early. It's like sitting in a dentist's waiting room: The sound of the drill in the next room and the time to reflect on it always make being in the chair seem worse than it really is.

Once the test is over, *it's over*. Although you may not feel perfectly satisfied (there's *always* room for improvement) you should not, like Sam, make a federal case out of it. **Once the pressure's off, relax, go out and have some fun.**

Life's Scenarios

Scenario #2: The Job Interview

"Hello, my name is Molly Landers. I have an appointment to see Mr. Davies."

"Yes, please have a seat, Miss Landers. Mr. Davies is in a meeting. He'll see you in a few minutes."

Molly glances at her watch: "But my appointment was at three . . ."

"If you're in a hurry, perhaps you should make another appointment."

"It's okay. I'll wait."

Twenty minutes later the interview begins. Here is a sampling of what transpires:

MR. DAVIES: I see you come highly recommended from art school. What kind of career do you see for yourself in graphic design?

MOLLY: Well, I believe I'm a very capable artist, but right now I want to learn more about the business end of it. My first priority is to find out what kinds of opportunities exist. At this point I'm mainly looking for a *successful* career.

MR. DAVIES: What are your salary requirements?

MOLLY: Well, I can't say I've given money much thought. What would you consider a fair salary?

MR. DAVIES: That depends . . . Now, just for my information, we have other positions open in the company—such as secretary in our personnel department, a bookkeeper in accounts payable. Would you be interested in either of these?

The Magic of Self-Confidence

MOLLY: No, I'm afraid they wouldn't be worth it to me. Graphic design is my field.

The interview ends, and Molly leaves after they've agreed that she'll check back in a week or so to see if a decision has been made.

ANALYSIS

Molly makes a mistake right off the bat. Always allow plenty of time in your schedule for an interview, but don't expect to be taken into the office right away. The interviewer may be under pressure himself, and your patience will be appreciated. If you have to wait a few minutes, do so graciously. Also, **always be polite to other employees:** They are as important to you as the interviewer is. A kind or unkind word from any one of them could tip the scales for or against you.

With one exception, Molly does well in the interview itself. She highlights her strengths without overselling herself. **Express your limitations honestly.** The employers I've talked to emphasize that they're looking for people with enthusiasm, people who express the desire to learn, and exhibit the confidence to do so. Molly is not prepared, however, when Mr. Davies brings up salary. Never answer an interviewer's question with another question—especially when it's a matter of money. Have a ballpark figure in mind (one you are prepared to negotiate) **before** you go to the interview; a direct answer shows you are serious about the job; it shows you have an idea of what your value to the company will be. (This is not to say you shouldn't feel free to ask questions of the interviewer. Inquiries about the company and your place in it will demonstrate your enthusiasm.)

Molly is right to take herself out of the running for the

Life's Scenarios

other jobs. **Never undervalue yourself.** Remember, *act* self-confident even when you don't *feel* so confident. Don't switch gears and accept another job until you have exhausted *all* the possibilities. Your patience, your determination, your qualifications will almost always pay off. Finally, like Molly, make sure you check back with the interviewer. Make it clear that you are available for follow-up interviews. It's much too easy to get lost in the shuffle of job seekers. **You are your own best publicity agent.**

The Magic of Self-Confidence

Scenario #3: Asking for a Raise

The second interview clicked and Molly got the job. After six months of working at the company and getting to know her co-workers, she realizes her mistake in not taking a firmer stand on salary. She knows she's underpaid, and heads straight for the boss's office.

MOLLY: I have a problem, Mr. Davies. Do you have a minute?

MR. DAVIES: What's up, Molly?

MOLLY: I can't make it on my salary, and now my landlord's raising the rent.

MR. DAVIES: The company's tightened the purse strings, Molly. We're all making sacrifices. Profits are down. Perhaps you should think about taking roommates.

MOLLY: I already have two. Furthermore, Donna and Steve both have the very same job as I do, and they both make more money than me!

MR. DAVIES: They've been with us longer than you, Molly. Listen, your annual salary evaluation comes up in just a few months. I'm going to do everything I can for you then.

MOLLY: I may have to start looking for another job before then, Mr. Davies.

MR. DAVIES: I'm sorry, Molly. I'm late for a meeting—let's talk later.

Life's Scenarios

ANALYSIS

Molly hasn't got a chance; every move she makes is the wrong one; she's pulled the rug out from under herself. Never rush in and ask for a raise impulsively. Give it careful consideration, work out your strategy, and **make an appointment.** It gives weight to your request, and it also denies your boss an escape hatch—he'll have to give you the chance to speak your piece.

Don't make the focus of your argument your financial difficulties. You are not a charity case—you're asking for just compensation for your work. Stress your dedication and your contributions to the company (making an appointment ahead of time allows you to prepare a presentation and have some examples of your work in mind). Then, in passing, you might mention that your cost of living has gone up. When asking for a raise think not only of your own needs, but of how you are responding to the company's needs.

Avoid, at all costs, comparing yourself to fellow employees. Your performance is the one that counts, in terms of both your value to the company and your self-esteem. Also avoid making threats unless you are prepared to carry them out. Suggesting that you might take another job is only an effective bargaining chip when you have the offers to back you up. If you don't have another offer, you're acting in desperation and your employer will know it. A competitive job bid puts you in the driver's seat; an empty threat puts him in it.

Molly's strategy now should be to start preparing immediately for her annual salary evaluation. She might work a few extra hours a week and start applying for work at other companies. Her goal here is to put herself in a stronger position, from her own standpoint and from the company's.

The Magic of Self-Confidence

Scenario #4: Salesmanship

Sam decides he wants to make a little extra cash. He studies, takes the test, and becomes a licensed real-estate agent hoping to sell a few houses. He's just gotten his first call: A couple is interested in looking at a $250,000 house just outside of town. Sam rushes out to meet them but, unfamiliar with the suburban streets, he's fifteen minutes late. The couple is waiting on the front lawn. He parks his car behind their Mercedes and gets out to greet them.

"So, I guess you've had a chance to see the grounds. Let's take a look inside."

"Can you tell us how far out the lot extends?"

"It's about an acre and a half or more. I don't know the exact dimensions, but I'll check them out when I get back to the office. One thing's for sure, though, you won't find another place like this, in this area, at this price. A real bargain."

Sam takes the couple inside and leads them through the house. On the way out the wife says, "This is the nicest property we've seen up to now, but we have a few more places to look at. Can we call you?"

"Sure, anytime. Listen, I have some other houses you might be interested in."

"Maybe another day. We have plenty to look at today."

"One thing to keep in mind," Sam concludes, "this one will go quickly. You should stay in touch."

ANALYSIS

Sam isn't applying the test-taking ability he showed us in scenario #1 to life's other situations. **Preparation and organization are the key to selling success.** As Sam is neither prepared nor organized, he loses the advantage.

Rule #1 of effective salesmanship is: **Know your prod-**

uct. Whether you're selling a used car for $1,000 or advertising space in a magazine at $10,000 a page, you are the one and only spokesperson for your product. If you don't describe its benefits, nobody will. By arriving late (Sam is selling real estate, which means he should know the surrounding neighborhood as well as the house itself) and by not having the answers to his customers' questions, Sam forfeits the opportunity to act as spokesperson for his product. He compounds the problem by constantly trying to get the couple to follow his lead. **Taking the initiative does not mean running the whole show. Guide your customers; don't push them.** If you push them, they'll tend to pull away.

Rule #2: **Know your customer.** Match your customer to the product. In this instance, Sam makes the mistake of describing the house as a bargain. People who drive a Mercedes and look at $250,000 homes may be shopping for bargains, but they certainly don't want to hear it from you. They *want* to hear how exclusive the property is—they're paying for privilege. "To tell you the truth, this is one of the more expensive houses on my list; but then not everyone chooses to live in a home as beautiful as this, or in a neighborhood as special. The owners might be convinced to come down a few thousand if the right buyers come along." Conversely, if you're running a garage sale, *bargain* is exactly the right word.

Rule #3: **Know when to cool it.** Sam makes two final errors: 1) He's too quick to offer to show the couple other houses and thus distract them from this one—a property in which they've already expressed an interest. 2) He makes the oldest sales pitch in the world: "Buy now, or you'll lose your chance." **The best salespeople are those who express confidence in their product, not desperation to sell it.**

The Magic of Self-Confidence

Scenario #5: The Sporting Life

Sam is a pretty good tennis player. He holds his own against most of his friends and wins as often as he loses—except when he plays his friend Rick. Sam's convinced that Rick is no better than he in the fundamentals of the game, but of their last thirty sets Sam has won maybe five. Lately he's been having second thoughts, going over the games in his head, reliving each missed shot, thinking that if he'd just hit this shot a little easier, that one a little harder he would have won going away. Last week, after yet another loss:

"Good game, Rick," Sam said, seething, wishing he could smash his tennis racket into the asphalt. "Same time next week?"

"Sure thing," Rick replied casually, as if he meant to imply it would be good practice for his *real* games. "Let me buy you a beer."

For this week's match, Sam's feeling more relaxed than usual; he's managed to put the preceding game out of his mind. Today he's not going to rush the net on every shot as he has in the past against Rick; he's going to play his own game, not force the action. As he begins to take practice serves, he concentrates on the sound of the ball meeting the strings of his racket, then on the sight of it whizzing across the net.

"Hey, Rick," Sam says just before they start, "I feel like hustling you today. Ten bucks to the winner—what do you say?"

ANALYSIS

I'd put my money on Sam. I think he has a fair chance of beating Rick this week. As frustrated and angry at himself as he was last week, he did not let go and show it.

Life's Scenarios

He maintained his composure. In many areas of life (especially competitive sports) **the way you are perceived is often as important as the way you feel.** *Acting* self-confident is one short step away from *being* self-confident. You *create* your Circle of Self-Confidence. (Actors never talk about *pretending* to be someone else, they talk about *becoming* someone else; the same principle applies.) Sam challenges Rick to another game, *as if* his losses haven't fazed him.

Sam has stopped rehashing the previous matches in his head (remember the labyrinth of the three Rs: reassessment, repetition, and regret?) and his mind is clear. Sports activity requires a mental state distinct from our usual one; all successful athletes experience it. It's a combination of concentration, physical intensity, and mental relaxation. It is thinking with your senses, with your eyes, with your body. If this concept intrigues you and you want to know more, refer to *The Inner Game of Tennis* by Timothy Galway.

One final note about Sam: Offering to make the bet with Rick adds a nice touch. **A psychological edge over an opponent can go a long way in sports.** Sam has given Rick food for thought—a perfectly fair way to distract him from his game. Sports contests are competitions of mind as well as body.

The Magic of Self-Confidence

Scenario #6: Getting Service with a Smile

Molly, who recently opened a small but gradually growing account at a new bank, has decided it would be helpful now and beneficial in the future if she had a line of credit. After depositing her paycheck during Friday's lunch hour, Molly goes to the bank officers' area and asks to see Mrs. Gold. Several customers later, Mrs. Gold motions to Molly to come to her desk.

"Hello, my name is Molly Landers. I'd like to apply for a line of credit. I have letters of recommendation from the personnel department of my company and from Mr. Davies, the director of my department. He suggested I talk to you, Mrs. Gold."

"Bill Davies has been a customer of ours for years. Do you have any credit references, Miss Landers?"

Molly shows Mrs. Gold the payment records from her car purchase several years back, and a note she asked her landlord to write attesting to the fact that she pays her rent on the first of every month. Mrs. Gold asks her to fill out an application.

"What do you think my chances are?" Molly asks as she gets up to leave. "I know credit is tight these days."

"We'll just have to wait and see."

ANALYSIS

Getting satisfactory service from any individual or institution can be a very tricky business. And as most of us have had occasion to find out, getting it from a bank can be excruciating. Bankers have particularly unpleasant reputations, and they often live up to them. Molly, however, with a few strategic blunders, does a commendable job.

The sad fact is, a person off the street has very little

chance in a bank. **If you want privileged service, arm yourself with plenty of information and contacts if possible.** Bring backup with you—whether it's from your family, your employer, your school, or even your friends. Banks are bureaucracies; the better you address the bureaucracy the more welcome you'll be. One mistake Molly makes is coming to see Mrs. Gold on Friday at lunch hour—she risks getting lost in that bureaucracy. Set yourself apart, make an appointment. If you're really determined to get a loan or open a line of credit, you might want to ask your banker to lunch. The better he or she knows you, the better your chances are of getting it. For a comprehensive guide to the banking obstacle course, I strongly recommend *All You Need to Know About Banks* (Bantam Books) by John A. Cook and Robert Wool. Mr. Cook is a former vice president of the Bank of New York and he knows what customers have to do to get results.

The golden rule when you're trying to get service is: **They need you more than you need them.** Remember, you can always pick up your money and go elsewhere; there are plenty of other fish in the sea. Never settle for less than service with a smile, which is your right as a customer. Also, don't be like Molly and ask what your chances are; always assume that you'll get what you're after. **The more confidence you have, the more confidence others will have in you.**

Scenario #7: The Party

One of Molly's friends from work has invited her to a party. Upon arriving, she finds that she doesn't know many of the people there, and so she sticks close to those few she does know. There is, however, one stranger at the party who attracts her attention—a nice-looking, apparently unattached man whom she'd like very much to meet. She's tempted to walk right up to him and introduce herself, but she holds back, waiting for an opportune moment. (She's thinking: If he's interested, *he'll* come over to *me* . . . I *have* to lose a few pounds!)

Every once in a while Molly glances in his direction, and as the night wears on she gets a feeling that he's glancing back. But she can't be absolutely sure. "Maybe he's got his eye on one of my friends," she thinks, and resolves to start a new diet tomorrow. Full of determination to turn over a new leaf, she goes to say good night to her hostess.

As it happens, the gentleman with whom Molly's been exchanging glances all evening is presently standing at the door saying good night as well.

"Oh, Molly, are you leaving already?" the hostess asks. "Have you met my brother, Sam?"

"No, no I haven't."

Molly and Sam shake hands, strike up a conversation, express an interest in getting to know one another, and exchange telephone numbers.

ANALYSIS

Molly and Sam should consider themselves very lucky; if it weren't for the fact that I like happy endings, they *never* would have gotten together. Even though each was interested in meeting the other, neither was

Life's Scenarios

willing to take the initiative, to take the kind of risk that leads to success and fulfillment. Taking a risk, in this sense, does not mean jumping out of an airplane or driving a race car; it means directing *all* your energies toward a desired goal—even if you know you may not reach it. **You'll never know for sure until you try.**

Molly's attitude when she first arrives at the party is a healthy one. She should stick close to her friends until she's at ease. Forcing yourself into a situation in which you feel uncomfortable can only make you more so. But once she's decided she wants to meet the man across the room, she should do everything she can to make it happen (the same, of course, goes for Sam). She *may* regret it once she does; but she'll *certainly* regret it if she doesn't. Molly would do well to follow her instincts; she shouldn't think too hard here, she shouldn't sell herself short. Just as in competitive sports, thinking too much can often be a hindrance in the interaction between the sexes. In a situation like this, act upon your feelings—that's what they're there for!

There are no narrators to create opportunities for you as I did for Molly and Sam. **You have to write your own story, you have to create your own opportunities.**

Scenario #8: Making the First Date

"Hello, Molly? This is Sam. We met at my sister's party the other night..."

"Oh, hi, Sam, how are you? I'm glad you called—I was going to call you."

"Listen, are you free Friday night? I thought you might come to my apartment for dinner. I'll make you one of my favorite pasta dishes, an old family recipe..."

"Sam, Friday's no good for me.... But what are you up to on Saturday? How about packing up some sandwiches and driving out to the beach? We could make a day of it, and it'll keep us both out of the kitchen."

"Sounds great. You bring the car, I'll bring the sandwiches. What kind of wine do you like, Molly?"

"Well, it depends on the sandwiches. White for chicken, red for peanut butter—I have a *very* sensitive palate. Really, anything's fine with me—red, white, beer... whatever."

"A woman after my own heart... So, do you want to come by and pick me up around ten?"

"Fine. I'm looking forward to it, Sam."

ANALYSIS

Sam and Molly are off to a good start. The toughest hurdle to get over is always that first phone call. Many people feel like they have to make a perfect first impression, or they'll blow the whole deal. It's simply not the case. First impressions are overrated. The other person is usually much more concerned about how *he* or *she* is coming across than about how *you* are.

The key is striking a balance. When asking for a first date, make it clear how much the idea appeals to you without sounding too anxious (your anxiousness may scare off your counterpart). Be flexible and accommodating, but don't just submit yourself to the other person's will—don't agree to do something you might later wish you hadn't. Molly wants to see Sam, but she wants to get to know him before she agrees to go to his apartment; consequently, she offers an alternative without putting him on the spot. Sam and Molly both seem to be at ease, and ready and willing to compromise. Don't enter into a conversation like this with your idea of how it should come out set in stone. **Give and take is essential.**

Try to put the other person at ease. The more relaxed he or she is, the more relaxed you'll be. Show your interest and enthusiasm. And when you speak, speak *to* the person—use his or her name. It creates an instant connection between the two of you, it breaks the ice. Once the ice is broken, the rest should start to flow smoothly. **The beauty of self-confidence is this: It opens doors for you without breaking them down.**

8
What Other Authors Have Written That Can Help You

In the classic movie *Miracle on 34th Street,* Macy's department store inadvertently hires a toy-department Santa Claus who, instead of hyping Macy's toys exclusively, sends the children and their parents to the store's competitors as well. His first concern, you see, is that the children get the toys they *really* want. Although Santa's technique goes against all of Macy's principles of salesmanship, it turns out to be a public relations bonanza, and Macy's business consequently skyrockets. The result is, everyone gets what they're after: The children get the best toys, the parents get happy children, and Macy's gets enhanced profits and public image. In that spirit of goodwill, recognizing that no single book can cover in depth every facet of self-confidence, I recommend several further readings.

I have narrowed the field down to the books of five authors. Together these seven titles comprise the best and most comprehensive writings available; each presents a unique perspective and expertise on a particular aspect of the magic of self-confidence. I describe them all in terms of what, specifically, they have to offer you. Now that this book has put you in the driver's seat, the others that follow are your road maps to many exciting new areas of self-exploration.

How to Win Friends and Influence People by Dale Carnegie

This is the granddaddy of them all, the Horatio Alger of self-confidence builders. First published in 1937, and having since sold over fifteen million copies in thirty-six different languages, it has for nearly fifty years provided sound and sensible advice to people in all walks of life—people who want to pull themselves up by the bootstraps and get down to the business of success in interpersonal relationships. Like a kindly relative, it is chock-full of common sense and uncommon wisdom. Here is a sampling of what it can show you:

- how to master the fundamental techniques of dealing with people
- how to make people like you, and how to make a first impression
- how to become a good conversationalist
- how to win people over to your way of thinking
- how to avoid making enemies
- how to be a leader

What Other Authors Have Written

- how to make people happy to do what you want them to do

These and many more nuggets of practical advice and inspirational insight—as relevant now as they were fifty years ago—make *How to Win Friends and Influence People* a compelling primer for everyone who wants to lead a fulfilling life at home and at work. It has stood the test of time.

(Available in hardcover from Simon & Schuster, and in paperback from Pocket Books.)

The Power of Positive Thinking by Norman Vincent Peale

The title tells it all. Norman Vincent Peale, one of the twentieth century's most influential spiritual leaders, expresses a great faith in the ability of us all to control our own destinies. He describes, in a simple, straightforward way, how you can harness your spiritual power and channel your mental energy in order to overcome personal problems and difficulties, and achieve the vitality and initiative you need to realize your hopes and ambitions. Based on the relaxation of body, mind, and spirit, Peale's technique is called "creative living."

The Power of Positive Thinking is a practical and thoughtful book that has been a source of inspiration and well-being to many. The principles outlined within are designed to help you experience a keen new pleasure in living, develop an inner strength, and become a person of expanded influence and deeper fulfillment.

I strongly recommend this book to the reader seeking reassurance and spiritual guidance. It will prove invaluable to anyone who feels oppressed by the complexity of life, or who desires help in coping with troubled times. *The Power of Positive Thinking* can give you the tools you need to master the magic of self-confidence.

(Available in hardcover from Prentice-Hall, and in paperback from Fawcett-Crest.)

I'm OK—You're OK by Thomas A. Harris

Anger, self-doubt, guilt, anxiety, and depression—often we feel crippled by our own emotions; they seem to stand in the way of achievement and success. Without knowing why, we hold ourselves back, erect barriers that appear impossible to cross. It's a kind of self-inflicted and irrational punishment—which is the worst kind, because it creates a vicious circle of anger and guilt.

I'm OK—You're OK cuts through the obscure theories and complicated meanings of psychoanalysis, and allows you to explore the inner workings of your mind and emotions. It helps you to discover why you act and feel the way you do, and enables you to change, to establish freedom of choice, self-control, and self-direction. By knowing yourself, according to Harris, you free yourself from the tyranny of your past and your upbringing. You break old patterns that have been with you from childhood, and, in a sense, become a new person.

If you find yourself fearful of intimacy in relationships, or of rising to greater responsibility in your career, *I'm OK—You're OK* may help you break through. Understanding yourself helps you to understand others, and is the first rung on the ladder of self-confidence.

(Available in hardcover from Harper & Row, and in paperback from Avon.)

What Other Authors Have Written

Passages and *Pathfinders* by Gail Sheehy

We never stop growing, developing, and changing. We confront new challenges—personally, socially, and sexually—at every stage of our lives. If we are prepared for those challenges, we can overcome them and also use them to our advantage—use them as opportunities for positive change.

In these two books Gail Sheehy guides you through the difficult passages from youth into adulthood, and from adulthood into middle age and beyond. She explores both the predictable *and* the unpredictable life crises, and how to smooth the transitions. She shows you the importance of risk-taking, how to make, break, or deepen life commitments, and how to reconcile your dreams and fantasies with your reality.

Taken together, *Passages* and *Pathfinders* are, in short, a road map of adult life. Through a creative process of self-formation, the author says, you can turn obstacles into opportunities. At every developmental stage of the life cycle, you can discover a renewal of purpose and achieve your full potential. Readers will find these books invaluable in dealing with each crisis—whether personal or professional—in their lives.

(*Passages* is available in hardcover from E. P. Dutton; *Pathfinders* from William Morrow & Co. Both are available in paperback from Bantam Books.)

Success and *Power* by Michael Korda

There are no more incisive or intelligent guides to corporate intrigue and the intricacies of office politics than these two books. If you are ready to climb the corporate ladder, ready to concentrate your energies on

The Magic of Self-Confidence

accomplishing your career goals, then these are the books for you. Insights include:

- how to get a raise, expense account, or promotion
- how to decipher the office pecking order and use it to your advantage
- how to proceed for success at office parties
- how to move in on and influence powerful people
- how to handle gossip
- how to frame your opinions for maximum effect
- how to seize the initiative and run with the ball of responsibility
- how to manipulate status symbols and use them to your advantage

Michael Korda is an expert on the corporate jungle; he knows it from the inside out. He understands the dynamics, the rules, and the rituals of power and success. He has an excellent feel for the psychological tricks and strategies that can give you the edge. If you're adept in the magic of self-confidence and ready to make your play for success and power, Korda tells you everything you need to know to meet the challenge and win. Give it your best shot!

(Both *Success* and *Power* are available in hardcover from Random House, and in paperback from Ballantine Books.)

9
Coming to Terms

If this is magic, let it be an art
Lawful as eating.
—WILLIAM SHAKESPEARE

The seeds of self-confidence are planted. The Circle has begun to spin.

There have been no sudden revelations, no drum rolls, no flourish of trumpets. The problems you had yesterday are still with you today, you still put your pants on, like everyone else, one leg at a time. But something's different, something *has* changed. Not overnight, but over time, those problems seem to have fallen into place. The tasks before you seem less a burden, more a challenge. The change is in the way you look at, in the way you see, in the way you respond to your environment—not in the environment itself.

A gradual process of reversal is under way:

No longer the victim of circumstances, you now perceive yourself as the creator of them.

The Magic of Self-Confidence

Once inclined toward passivity, you now tend toward action.

A world of impediments has become a world of possibilities.

With your newfound sense of authority has come a newfound sense of freedom. You feel a little bit relieved, a little bit excited—a little bit afraid. The fear of how it will affect you, the fear of losing it, the fear that at midnight it will turn back into a pumpkin . . . these sensations tell you that this new sense of freedom is something worth having.

You are ready to come to terms with the magic of self-confidence—ready to discover that the glass slipper fits!

To grow and thrive, to become an integral part of you, the seeds of self-confidence require supervision and nourishment. You want the Circle to spin, but not out of control. What we are concerned with here is that the grounds of your self-confidence not go fallow. We are concerned with the care and feeding of your newfound sense of authority.

When you decided to read this book you made a contract with yourself: You resolved to impress yourself upon the world, to carve out of it your rightful share. You contracted to fuel up your engines and revolutionize your life. But unless you occasionally renew the contract, the force behind it will expire.

Don't expect self-confidence to grow and thrive on its own. Let the magic be as fundamental, and as much a part of you, as eating. Thus will the force be with you today, tomorrow, and in the years to come. The force of your feelings and the freedom to acknowledge them. . . . The force of your beliefs and the courage to express them. . . . The force of your ambitions and the determination to realize them. . . . The force of your dreams and the will to follow them.

Coming to Terms

There will always be moments of self-doubt, moments of irresolution and of real and apparent failure. You will wake up one morning and not have the energy to get out of bed, let alone the ambition to conquer the world. You will feel trapped and alienated in your work life, unfulfilled in your personal life. We are all subject to the slings and arrows of outrageous fortune, and every now and again, they *do* hit the mark.

You will need to renew the contract. You will need a fallback position, something to help you get through the night, which brings us to terms . . .

The Ten Terms of the Self-Confidence Contract

1. PROPORTION

Maintain a sense of perspective and proportion in all your endeavors. What seems to be the most monumental obstacle, the most devastating setback when you are standing beside it, becomes less and less consequential as you distance yourself from it. Don't let problems and setbacks block out the light of reason. The human mind is like a magnifying glass: It exaggerates. A simple rule of thumb: Whatever you're looking at is not as big a deal as you think it is.

2. PERSEVERANCE

Perseverance is power. Don't give up. Go the distance and give it everything you've got. Rome wasn't built in a day, and neither will be your career, your fortune, or your love life. Thomas Edison said genius is "1 percent inspiration, and 99 percent perspiration," so sweat it out over the rough spots, and smooth sailing will follow. *I* say if you want something badly enough, you have to give it *100 percent*—you have to be willing to see it through, often with blood, sweat, and tears.

3. PREPARATION

To know something is to surround it, to take possession of it and make it yours. Preparation gives you control over a situation; it gives you the strength of will to follow through. Three words to the wise: practice, practice, practice. The road to success is not a race track, it's a curving, twisting, sometimes treacherous country lane. More important than speed is a feel for the territory and a good, solid grip on the wheel.

4. FOCUS

Concentrate all your energies on the task or situation at hand. You have at your disposal the two most marvelously devised and efficient machines ever created: the human body and the human mind. When used correctly, they can work wonders. They can move mountains. *You* can move mountains. Like a sprinter surging toward the finish line, focus every particle of yourself on your objective. Don't look back; surge ahead!

5. EXPERTISE

Make yourself an expert. Once you have found an area of special interest, learn as much about it as you possibly can. Nothing can boost your confidence—or open more doors for you—like knowing a subject better than the next guy. People admire, reward, and pay for expertise. From knowledge comes authority, and from authority come the privileges and prerogatives of power.

6. RESPONSIBILITY

The Cirle of Self-Confidence runs on responsibility. *Take* responsibility, and people will *give* you responsibility. Take responsibility for your health and well-being. Take responsibility for your work. Take responsibility for

Coming to Terms

your life, the good *and* the bad. Take responsibility, and you take the lead! Feel good about yourself and others will feel good about *you*. Be the kind of person people can count on, and it will pay off tomorrow!

7. SELF-AWARENESS
Know what you can do, know what you can't. Know your strengths, know your weaknesses. Know when to go it alone, know when to seek advice. Know when to conserve energy, know when to expend it. Know when to push forward, know when to pull back. Know what you want out of life—and know the pleasure of getting it!

8. IMAGE
Be image-conscious. Your demeanor—the way you look, act, and express yourself—is your calling card; it's what you leave behind, it's what people remember you by. *Act* self-confident, and you will *be* self-confident.

9. SPIRIT
Listen to your hopes, dreams, and desires, and follow where they lead you. If you're not enjoying the game, there's no point in playing it. Open up, take a risk, explore new possibilities in your life. Seek to refresh and revive your spirit of enthusiasm, your spirit of adventure. Life is a banquet: Feast on it!

10. MAGIC
We have come full circle. Remember always, the magic of self-confidence is within you. Exercise it, nurture it, delight in it. You have come to terms. You can make it happen. You have the power to achieve success.